To Sarah
Love Debbie
2016.

A Woman's Prayers
from the Heart

Publications International, Ltd.

Christine A. Dallman is a freelance writer living near Everett, Washington. She is the author of *Daily Devotions for Seniors*, an inspirational resource for maturing adults, as well as coauthor of several other Publications International, Ltd., titles.

Marie D. Jones is the author of several best-selling nonfiction books and a contributing author to numerous inspirational books, including *A Mother's Daily Prayer Book, When You Lose Someone You Love: A Year of Comfort,* and six books from the Echoes of Love series: *Sisters, Mother, Grandmother, Friends, Graduation,* and *Wedding.* She can be reached at www.mariedjones.com.

Louis Weber, CEO
Publications International, Ltd.
7373 North Cicero Avenue
Lincolnwood, Illinois 60712

ISBN-13: 978-1-4508-6368-1
ISBN-10: 1-4508-6368-X

Manufactured in China.

8 7 6 5 4 3 2 1

Library of Congress Control Number: 2012951325

A Woman's Prayers
from the Heart

Publications International, Ltd.

Christine A. Dallman is a freelance writer living near Everett, Washington. She is the author of *Daily Devotions for Seniors*, an inspirational resource for maturing adults, as well as coauthor of several other Publications International, Ltd., titles.

Marie D. Jones is the author of several best-selling nonfiction books and a contributing author to numerous inspirational books, including *A Mother's Daily Prayer Book*, *When You Lose Someone You Love: A Year of Comfort*, and six books from the Echoes of Love series: *Sisters*, *Mother*, *Grandmother*, *Friends*, *Graduation*, and *Wedding*. She can be reached at www.mariedjones.com.

Louis Weber, CEO
Publications International, Ltd.
7373 North Cicero Avenue
Lincolnwood, Illinois 60712

Permission is never granted for commercial purposes.

ISBN-13: 978-1-4508-6368-1
ISBN-10: 1-4508-6368-X

Manufactured in China.

8 7 6 5 4 3 2 1

Library of Congress Control Number: 2012951325

God, who lovingly calls you into companionship with him.

Whether *A Woman's Prayers from the Heart* becomes a go-to treasure on your bookshelf or a gem passed among friends, may you be blessed in some way by the role it plays in supporting and strengthening your relationship with our loving God.

CHAPTER 1

Receiving God's Daily Guidance

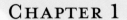

Lead me in Your truth and teach me,
For You are the God of my salvation;
On You I wait all the day.

—Psalm 25:5 NKJV

Father, I'm grateful that you cannot be taken off guard—that you see my life from the beginning to the end, and every step in between. Things may take me by surprise or disappoint me, but at the end of the day,

I can quiet my soul and entrust myself to you, because you knew what I needed all along. You have a plan in place to see me through. Thank you for always walking beside me, showing me the way to navigate each valley, each mountain, each obstacle, and each juncture.

I'll never stop looking to you to show me the way.

My lord knows the way
through the wilderness,
All I have to do is follow.
Strength for the day
is mine all the way
And all that I need for tomorrow.
My lord knows the way
through the wilderness,
All I have to do is follow.

—SIDNEY E. COX, "MY LORD KNOWS
THE WAY THROUGH THE WILDERNESS"

Your Word is my guidebook, Lord. From within its pages you show me when my thoughts and intentions are straying off the path, and you also assure me when I am doing right, helping me stay on course. I've heard some folks say they've already read the Bible, like it's already under their belt, so to speak. I wonder about that. I guess I'm a student who requires a lot of review, because I always feel a need to be reminded of your ways and refreshed in your truth. Thank you for the access I have to the scriptures. I know it hasn't always been so for previous generations. I feel humbled and blessed to be able to open up those amazing pages and read at will.

Your word is a lamp for my feet, a light on my path.

—PSALM 119:105 NIV

$\mathscr{I}$t's such a good thing to know that your guidance is something I can pass along to friends who ask me for advice. Each person is so different, each journey is unique, but your Word offers principles that translate universally across time and culture, personality and situation. It's not that a specific thing I did will work for someone else; instead it's the general approach to things—honesty, integrity, forgiveness, kindness, patience, etc.—that works no matter what, where, or when.

Human nature and human needs have not changed one iota over the centuries, and since God's understanding of these things is complete, his guidance will always be apt—simply timeless.

If I had to choose a slogan to sum up how following your guidance has worked out for me, I think the T-shirt or bumper sticker I'd be touting would say, "No regrets." I think back on the times I have chosen to take the faith route and trust that your direction was right, despite how foreign it seemed to my natural inclination, and I just want to shout, YES! It has always been the right choice, always the best decision, to follow your lead. And the more I choose that path of trusting you, the easier it becomes to choose it the next time. Thank you for being so faithful in teaching me your paths of truth and love. They have saved me from many pitfalls and prisons of my own making. They have led me down regret-free roads.

I have hidden your word in my heart that I might not sin against you.

—Psalm 119:11 NIV

Contents

Heart to Heart with God

As women, we often lead hectic, full lives with little downtime. *A Woman's Prayers from the Heart* is a book that will help us slow down, take a moment with God, and gather strength for our day. The prayers in this book echo the thoughts and feelings that rise up from a woman's heart—from sorrow to gratitude and from loneliness to love. For further reflection, the prayers are supplemented by quotes and Bible verses.

Individual prayers are brief enough to read in a minute or two, providing food for thought throughout the day. Or you may want to peruse an entire chapter at a time, focusing on the most relevant prayer or prayers for your situation. This prayer book can adapt to your personal needs.

There are ten chapters to choose from, and the prayers in each chapter are intended to draw you into dialogue with an ever-present, approachable

Contents

Heart to Heart with God

As women, we often lead hectic, full lives with little downtime. *A Woman's Prayers from the Heart* is a book that will help us slow down, take a moment with God, and gather strength for our day. The prayers in this book echo the thoughts and feelings that rise up from a woman's heart—from sorrow to gratitude and from loneliness to love. For further reflection, the prayers are supplemented by quotes and Bible verses.

Individual prayers are brief enough to read in a minute or two, providing food for thought throughout the day. Or you may want to peruse an entire chapter at a time, focusing on the most relevant prayer or prayers for your situation. This prayer book can adapt to your personal needs.

There are ten chapters to choose from, and the prayers in each chapter are intended to draw you into dialogue with an ever-present, approachable

Following your guidance can be a lot like flying an airplane on a dark cloudy night with only the instrument panel to rely on. There are times when I can't see the ground beneath me, I can't see the horizon in front of me, I can't see the stars or the moon above me—there's nothing familiar by which to navigate. With all my normal reference points out of sight, I'm left to trust in the promptings of your Spirit, which remind me of the truth of your Word. These are the very instruments I need to keep flying straight, and they never fail.

When we're forced to "fly" by faith
and not by sight, we're learning to trust in
new ways that defy what our mistaken instincts
or misguided feelings are shouting to us.
It's a powerful trust-building experience.

*Lord, when I wake, the first two things I realize
are that you are with me and a new day is before
me. Help me be mindful, then, that you have
given me a fresh opportunity to live well . . .
maybe to make some changes and certainly to
follow you more closely. I'm grateful for these new
beginnings and for the wisdom and direction that
you so willingly supply to guide me into what is
right and true and good.*

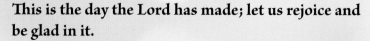

This is the day the Lord has made; let us rejoice and be glad in it.

—PSALM 118:24

Too often it feels as if I'm being pulled in a dozen directions, Lord. Please help me stop and ask myself, "Who am I allowing to guide me right now?" Your voice is the one I want to listen and respond to. Teach me how to filter out the mere noise and hear only what is essential to living within your heart of truth and love. Then help me speak up and say "Yes" to what you want and "No" to everything else.

The power of a word
Makes or breaks my freedom;
The power of a word
Can turn my world around
If I say it like it is:
No or yes, yes or no.
Truth in love,
The power of . . . a word.

—CHRISTINE DALLMAN, "THE POWER OF A WORD"

Father, when there is a big decision for me to make and everyone around me is telling me what they think I should do—but something within me is giving me pause—help me not to give in to the majority opinion just because it seems like nine out of ten friends can't possibly be wrong. Instead, when the pressure's on and my soul is not at peace, help me have the courage to wait for your Spirit to bring the clarity I need to move forward with confidence.

Sometimes the lack of certainty about
a situation we're facing is the guidance
we need in the moment to cause us to pause
and wait. God's direction in our lives is
often as much about timing and waiting
as it is about moving and doing.

Father, help me move forward and not be afraid to
fail. Sometimes it's in the trying and failing that you
teach us more than we ever could have learned from a
string of successes. You're teaching me that you don't
measure success and failure the way we humans do.
To trust in ourselves in a way that causes us to forget
you is the path to pride and spiritual failure. But to
trust you is ultimate success in any situation. Help me
fearlessly follow you and trust you whether it seems
like I'm flying or faltering.

The writer of Hebrews asserted that without faith it is *impossible* to please God. So we know that God is well pleased with those who trust him . . . and who keep on trusting him through all the ups and downs of life.

For this is God,
Our God forever and ever;
He will be our guide
Even to death.

—PSALM 48:14 NKJV

Lord Jesus, I'm so grateful that I belong to you! To know you look out for me is a great comfort as I move along this path of life. I know I'm not a meaningless mote of dust in the wind. I am your beloved child— a lamb in your sheepfold. I matter to you. If I stray from the path, you call me back. If I become lost and call out to you, you rescue me. You are the one who provides what I need, tends to my wounds, speaks truth to me, and leads me all the days of my life.

We are Thine, do Thou befriend us,
be the guardian of our way;
Keep Thy flock, from sin defend us,
seek us when we go astray.
Blessed Jesus, blessed Jesus!
Hear, O hear us when we pray.
Blessed Jesus, blessed Jesus!
Hear, O hear us when we pray.

—DOROTHY ANN THRUPP,
"SAVIOR, LIKE A SHEPHERD LEAD US"

Heavenly Father, when I face big decisions, I am often afraid to move forward. When I feel paralyzed by indecision, remind me that no matter which job I take or which town I move to or which house I live in, you are with me. Thank you that your will for my life doesn't ultimately lie in particulars but rather in the forming of my character to become more like you. That's the direction I need always be moving. Thank you for leading me in your path of righteousness.

We may wonder, "What is God's will for my life?" as if it were a series of "right" places to be and "right" work to be doing. But God's big-picture will is that we learn to love him and be loved by him. From within that loving relationship, then, he often allows us freedom to decide where we will live and work as we grow in our relationship with him.

And when you turn to the right or when you turn to the left, your ears shall hear a word behind you, saying, "This is the way; walk in it."

—Isaiah 30:21

Lord, my days are filled with so many different kinds of choices! There are at least a dozen laundry soaps I can choose from at the store. There are several different ways I might order my day. There are choices to make about my budget. And there are times when I feel myself pausing in a conversation, wondering whether to say a certain thing or not. I realize that some of these choices matter more than others—some have to do with what's right and wrong, while others are just about preferences and druthers. As I consider this, I need your guidance each day to help me discern, moment-to-moment, when I am at a juncture that matters and when I should carefully choose what to say or do next.

I have a friend whose rule to live by when faced with a difficult choice is "Do the next right thing." When what is right is apparent, the choice becomes simple (though not always easy). "But," she tells me, "doing the next right thing leaves me with fewer regrets and better sleep at night."

*L*ord, the older I get, the more challenging I find it to make big changes in my life. Transitions can be great stressors, but I know they can also turn into wonderful opportunities. Help me have eyes of hope and a heart of anticipation so that I can turn my face toward the changes you bring and smile at them, even as I may be grieving the loss of some of the old things. Remind me that you are already there in the changes, that you have ample grace and comfort for me along the way as I learn to trust you in my new circumstances.

**The Lord will guide you continually,
And satisfy your soul in drought,
And strengthen your bones;
You shall be like a watered garden,
And like a spring of water, whose waters do not fail.**

—Isaiah 58:11 NKJV

"Notion your mind with the idea that
God is there. If once the mind is notioned
along that line, then when you are in difficulties,
it is as easy as breathing to remember—
Why, my Father knows all about it!"

—Oswald Chambers, *My Utmost for His Highest*

Father, I understand from reading your Word that just as the heavens are higher than the earth, so your thoughts are higher than my thoughts and your ways better than my ways. I just want to tell you right now how grateful I am that you have not left me to muddle about in my own thoughts and ways. I chuckle (and sometimes cringe) when I think of the situational pickles I've gotten myself into when doing my own thing. I want to thank you that you don't just stand above me with your great thoughts and ways, shaking your head, but that in your uniquely kind and gentle approach, you offer your wisdom and guidance whenever I look to you and ask for help.

God reveals his greatness to us not
to intimidate us, but to invite us to trust
in him more than we already do.

If any of you lacks wisdom, let him ask of God, who gives to all liberally and without reproach, and it will be given to him. But let him ask in faith, with no doubting, for he who doubts is like a wave of the sea driven and tossed by the wind.

—JAMES 1:5–6 NKJV

Father, I'm realizing that leaning into you is truly trusting you. I'm seeing that praying for more strength to face the day so that I can go it alone is missing my opportunity to lean into your strength that lifts me up, even carries me. And in that leaning, Lord, the relationship grows between us as my trust in you deepens. Please help me lean into you more fully today, finding fellowship with you as you give me your wisdom and strength along this path of life.

Trust in the Lord with all your heart and lean not on your own understanding; in all your ways submit to him, and he will make your paths straight.

—Proverbs 3:5–6 NIV

Father, help me remember how willing you are to give me the direction and wisdom I need to get through each day. Help me learn to seek you in prayer as a first resort for the questions I have or challenges I face, rather than running to you only when I'm worried or at my wit's end. You and I both know how I go a little too far in my tendency to try doing things on my own. If nothing else, maybe the motivation of slowing down any gray hairs will help me change my ways! How well you know me, Father, and how kindly you look after me. Thank you for guiding me.

Ask and it will be given to you; seek and you will find; knock and the door will be opened to you. For everyone who asks receives; the one who seeks finds; and to the one who knocks, the door will be opened.

—Matthew 7:7–8 NIV

As I spend time with you, Lord, in prayer and in your Word, I learn more about who you are and what you are like. It changes me, moves my perspective closer to the truth, and it transforms the way I understand how you work in my life. Please continue to disclose yourself to me as I learn to follow your direction and trust your guidance. It's a process I look forward to continuing all the days of my life.

We learn about guidance primarily by learning about the Guide. It is the knowledge of God and His ways with men which ultimately gives us stability in doing His will.

—SINCLAIR B. FERGUSON, *DISCOVERING GOD'S WILL*

Thank you for the wise people in my life, Lord Jesus, who offer insight as I consider what I should do right now. But now I want to bring all of the thoughts and opinions they offered to you. I need your help in sifting through what is worth keeping and what I should leave behind. I know your Word is a perfect filter and that your Spirit will lead me into all truth, as you promised he would. It may take some time, but I am certain you will guide me to a good decision.

A person once told me, "When I give you advice, treat it like eating fish: Digest what is helpful, and then throw away the bones."

The Spirit of the Lord will rest on him—
the Spirit of wisdom and of understanding,
the Spirit of counsel and of might,
the Spirit of the knowledge and fear of the Lord.

—ISAIAH 11:2 NIV

Father, I admit that I turn some things that should be "no-brainers" into "rocket science projects" when it comes to your daily guidance. There are some things that you tell me clearly in your Word, but in my desire to skirt around the truth, I manage all kinds of mental gymnastics and contortions to find a different answer. Please forgive me for turning my back on your clear instructions in my attempt to rewrite your will. Help me trust that the guidelines you have in place truly are for my benefit and not to deprive me of happiness. (You've proved as much over time.) Help me believe you—not second-guess you.

If we believe our Creator knows us completely and loves us fully, then he certainly has our best interest at heart, as well as the wisdom to accomplish the best outcome for us.

The guide is the one who leads, right, Father? Then why do I find myself running ahead of you so often? I see something I want, and I just start running for it. I'm a lot like a kid who sees an ice cream truck across the street and runs into the road without thinking. My impulsive ways are not just foolish but also dangerous, aren't they? Thank you for all the times you've saved me from myself. I know there is a wiser, safer way, and I'm on it when I'm right on the heels of my faithful guide—you.

Sometimes we find ourselves needing God's guidance out of a sticky situation that our impulsive decision-making has gotten us into. God is always willing to help us get back on track.

Today I want to spend time with you, Renewing Spirit. In fact, I'd like to spend the whole day just being in your presence. For this one day I will not worry about the work I have to do or the goals I want to accomplish. I will pull back and simply listen for your guidance. I'm willing to change my life in order to fit your perfect will, and I ask that you begin that work in my heart. I'll let go of personal ambition, for now. I'll loosen my grip on the things I've wanted to accomplish and the recognition I've craved for so long. All of this I give over to you. I'm content to be a servant for now, quiet and unnoticed, if that is what you desire. I'm even willing to be misunderstood, if you will only respond to my sincere prayer for a renewed heart. Thank you. I need you so much.

Ah, what solace there is in your promise of peace. True help and real peace are to be found from trusting in your guidance and inspiration.

**The humble He guides in justice,
And the humble He teaches His way.
All the paths of the Lord are mercy and truth,
To such as keep His covenant and His testimonies.**

—Psalm 25:9–10 NKJV

So here I am, waiting. I have answered your call to pray. I have heard your guidance—to sit tight. I have chosen quiet and rest because that is your will for me now. I am sitting on the sidelines, watching the hectic pace around me. I am finding contentment in the little blessings that flow into my days. I am trying to see all these things as big blessings because they come from you. But when can I get going again?

When will I do the great works I've envisioned? When will the situation require dedicated action once again? When will I hear the trumpet call? When will I finally move onward and upward? I'm ready, Great Spirit! Here I am . . . waiting.

When I feel my control slipping, Lord,
I know I only have to call on you for
encouragement, direction, and guidance
to get your loving assistance.

CHAPTER 2

Finding Peace
in the Storm

The Lord blesses his people
with peace.

—Psalm 29:11 NIV

46

God's Spirit offers us the
blessing of inner peace.

*W*hen the circumstances of my life feel like a storm
is blowing through—uprooting, flooding, twisting,
burying—I can feel myself getting frantic, Father.
I want to be able to do something to stop it, but I am
powerless to change the course of something so beyond
my control. And it's only when I stop flailing and
grasping like a drowning swimmer that I realize I am
being held by you, that you have not left me to brave
the elements on my own. Whatever may be damaged,
lost, or destroyed is also in your hands, and you are
the one who restores, heals, and redeems, if only
I will give you time to show me.

When peace like a river attendeth my way,
When sorrows like sea-billows roll;
Whatever my lot, Thou has taught me to say,
"It is well, it is well with my soul."

—HORATIO GATES SPAFFORD,
"IT IS WELL WITH MY SOUL"

Dear Lord, some people are like stormy weather that can cloud up fair skies in a hurry. Just the sight of them entering a room can make me wish I could crawl into a cave until the storm of their words and ways passes by. I don't like feeling this way about anyone. I don't want to hide. I want to be like a warm sunshine set in a bright blue sky that either wins them over or chases them away. I pray that your spirit of love, joy, peace, patience, kindness, goodness, faithfulness, gentleness, and self-control would be just that in my life, and that your peace would prevail in each "human storm" that comes my way.

When a woman of faith has a sense of knowing who she is and what she is about, her inner peace and beauty are like a brilliant light, drawing people to the truth and love she lives in.

My own failures, foibles, and flaws are like storms of shame and frustration that recur regularly in my life, Lord. That's why I want to learn to look at them from your perspective. How do you see those things? It seems as though they tether me to you, reminding me of my need for your grace and mercy and love. They keep me from wandering too far away from you in arrogant self-assurance. They remind me to be gentle with others who are struggling. They are opportunities to grow. They nurture the peaceful quality of humility in my life. Next time I stumble, Lord, remind me of these things. Keep me from letting unnecessary storms ruin the day you have made for me to rejoice in.

God is a great redeemer. He can turn our worst mistakes into ultimate blessings when we come to him with a humble, truthful heart.

Uncertainty about the future seems to be at an all-time high, Father. I don't know what to think about the storm that may be brewing on the horizon. It feels like the peace and security we've grown accustomed

to are being threatened on so many
fronts, and I'm not sure who to
believe anymore. You don't need
me to write the list. You know
all the ways things are unraveling.
I just need to take my eyes off all
the craziness for a while and look at
you again. That's where I'll find the
peace of remembering that you are
moving things toward your ultimate
plan. Those who trust in you will be
kept safe.

[Jesus said,] "I have told you these things, so that in
me you may have peace. In this world you will have
trouble. But take heart! I have overcome the world."

—JOHN 16:33 NIV

In His will is our peace.

—Dante Alighieri

I can picture the satellite hurricane pictures, Father. They show a huge swirling pattern of dangerous weather. But right in the center, there is an eye— a place of perfect peace. If a person could remain in that eye, even though there are deadly winds blowing all around them, they could ride out the storm unharmed. To me, Father, the world is one of those storms, and you are like the eye. Please hold me, carry me, keep me where your peace remains at all times, no matter what is going on around me.

[Jesus said,] "Peace I leave with you; my peace I give you. I do not give to you as the world gives. Do not let your hearts be troubled and do not be afraid."

—JOHN 14:27 NIV

I admit that the slightest distraction can pull my mind out of its orbit around you, Father. You know how I am: I can be praying or praising you one minute, and the next moment a phone call with some disturbing news or maybe a careless driver cuts me off on the road and POOF!—my peace has left the building, and I'm all out of sorts. I want to ask you, though, to help me. I want to grow into a more steadfast frame of mind— one that can take the bad news and thoughtless people of life in stride, acknowledging them for what they are, but not allowing them to rock my world. Would you help me take a step in that direction today? Thank you, Father.

You will keep in perfect peace those whose minds are steadfast, because they trust in you.

—ISAIAH 26:3 NIV

Prayer opens the door to peace.

Sometimes I begin to slip into the illusion that I am in control of my world, Father. I imagine that I can arrange things just the way I like them and that I can create my own peace by making sure everyone and everything follows my plan. Oh, how that house of cards gets blown away in the winds of adversity! How quickly I am reminded that I cannot manufacture

*peace with manipulation. You are my peace. You are
my source of well-being, safety, and security. Apart
from you there is no true peace to be had.*

God cannot give us a happiness
and peace apart from Himself, because it is
not there. There is no such thing.

—C. S. LEWIS, *MERE CHRISTIANITY*

When the storms of life are raging around me, I need to remind myself about you, Father. The news I hear of what's going on in the world can be disturbing,

but just a walk or drive outdoors can remind me that you are still the one who makes the sun rise and set, who causes life to spring up from the earth, who orders both the orbitals of atomic particles and the orbits of galaxies. The changing of the seasons reminds me of the intricate plan you have set in

motion for maintaining life on earth and your faithfulness in carrying it out from generation to generation. I'm reminded again that although the freedom you grant us in this life means that some people will make terrible choices, the truth of your goodness remains constant. All who take refuge in you and trust in you enjoy ultimate peace.

No amount of bad news can change the truth about the Good News—the eternal Gospel of peace with God through Christ.

But the meek will inherit the land and enjoy peace and prosperity.

—PSALM 37:11 NIV

Everyone around me is upset, Father. I could get carried away in this emotional upheaval, but I realize I need to get away and spend some time with you to find a better approach. Only you can show me how to navigate this with sensitivity and strength. Your wisdom transcends the options I see and can show me things I didn't think of. Your Spirit knows the heart and mind of each person involved in this, and only you can guide me in my response to each one. Thank you that I can come to you and find a refuge in your peace and then carry that peace into my responses.

The peace we carry away from our times with God is a balm we can carry into a troubled world.

Now may the Lord of peace himself give you peace at all times in all ways. The Lord be with all of you.

—2 Thessalonians 3:16

Lord, I am overwhelmed! There is too much for me to handle right now. My soul feels like a lead weight, my heart is despondent, and my mind is numb. I want to escape, to run away or just shut down, but there are things before me that I simply must do. Please help me! I need to be carried by you, to be carried into your peace, with the assurance that all of this will not be the end of me, but that you will lift me up and show me the way through it.

From the end of the earth I will cry to You,
When my heart is overwhelmed;
Lead me to the rock that is higher than I.

—PSALM 61:2 NKJV

Father, I've noticed that when I make my primary objective to treat people with kindness and respect (instead of focusing on our different beliefs, values, and opinions), there is a level of respect I receive in return. Even people who might be religious or political enemies, so to speak, are inclined to permit me my perspectives without being antagonistic. It's even true that zealous would-be opponents will sometimes treat me favorably, not because I water down what I believe in but because your love can have that effect on people. And when your love touches our lives, it subdues animosity and fosters peace. Thank you for showing me how good your command is to love my neighbor as myself.

When the ways of people please the Lord, he causes even their enemies to be at peace with them.

—PROVERBS 16:7

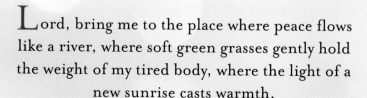

Lord, bring me to the place where peace flows like a river, where soft green grasses gently hold the weight of my tired body, where the light of a new sunrise casts warmth.

I notice such a difference in how my day goes when I take some quiet time out to pray and fix my thoughts on you, Lord. It sets the tone for everything that follows, and even if I get distracted or off track at some point, it's much easier to reconnect to that peaceful place of fellowship with you when I've started my day there. Please draw me back every day to this quiet sanctuary of prayer and meditation on your Word.

Spiritual nourishment must come as regularly to
us as the food we eat to nourish our bodies.
We grow spiritually weaker or stronger,
depending on how regularly we take in God's
Word and take time to be with him in prayer.

In hope that sends a shining ray
far down the future's broad'ning way,
in peace that only thou canst give,
with thee, O Master, let me live.

—WASHINGTON GLADDEN,
"O MASTER, LET ME WALK WITH THEE"

**Let the peace of Christ rule in your hearts....
And be thankful.**

—COLOSSIANS 3:15

*L*earning what your Word says has brought so much clarity to my life, so much certainty about how I can live well and enjoy my relationship with you and know how to navigate my relationships with others. Living within your truth brings increased freedom and peace, not constriction and misery, as I used to fear when I was younger. Thank you for opening my understanding and for blessing my experience with the peace of walking in your ways. I love your law—your truth—and when I follow you in it, I never miss a step.

Great peace have those who love your law, and nothing can make them stumble.

—Psalm 119:165 NIV

Being able to entrust those I love most to your care lifts a burden of worry from my soul, Father. As I bring my concerns for them to you in prayer, it's as if I transfer my responsibility for them over to you, in whom all the help they need truly lies. Help me remember that my worry cannot change one reality in their lives; your daily loving influence on their hearts and minds, however, certainly can. You can see and protect them when I cannot. You can speak to them and call to them in ways I never could. And you love them even more than I do. To find peace of mind, that's something I need to remember as you watch over those closest to my heart.

Like a river glorious, is God's perfect peace,
Over all victorious, in its bright increase;
Perfect, yet it floweth, fuller every day,
Perfect, yet it groweth, deeper all the way.
Stayed upon Jehovah, hearts are fully blest
Finding, as He promised, perfect peace and rest.

—Frances Havergal, "Like a River Glorious"

The mind governed by the Spirit is life and peace.

—ROMANS 8:6 NIV

Lord, you are teaching me that finding peace requires me to seek it out—to look for and pursue peaceful places, peaceful ways, and peaceful relationships. If I make living in peace a priority, I won't miss the chaos, and even when storms come my way I will know where to find rest and calm and quietude of spirit. Your Word so often pairs righteousness and peace. To live uprightly is to live in peace. Help me, Lord, choose what is right and true and good today, as I seek to live in your peace.

**Consider the blameless, observe the upright;
a future awaits those who seek peace.**

—PSALM 37:37 NIV

The Serenity Prayer that is so often quoted, Father, reminds me to discern between the things I can and cannot change, and it challenges me to focus on the things I can change. It seems you are showing me that the only things I have the ability to change are those that have to do with myself. It's so hard to give up trying to change other people. You keep reminding me that I lose peace trying, so I know I need to surrender my will to yours. Let peace be found in seeing the changes you make in my life as I focus on following you.

God give us grace to accept with serenity the things that cannot be changed, courage to change the things that should be changed, and wisdom to distinguish the one from the other.

—Reinhold Niebuhr

While we can influence others,
we can change only ourselves.

What happens if someone doesn't want to be at peace with me, Father? How do I find peace when they are always at war, stirring up conflict? What do I do? Ignore them? Placate them? Set up boundaries? Escape? There may be no easy answers, but I pray you will give me your grace and wisdom to do what is best for now until you bring relief or show me the way out. Please shelter me from the "bombs" being lobbed at me. May I find my peace in your goodness to me.

**If it is possible, as far as it depends on you,
live at peace with everyone.**

—ROMANS 12:18 NIV

Help me turn off the noise, Father: the radio, the television, the imaginary conversations I'm having in my mind, the texting, the e-mailing, the phone calls. Help me quiet my mind, quiet my heart, quiet my spirit; I need to settle down into your peace. The peace of prayer and the peace of being with you are great healers in my stressed-out life. So I need to stop, wind down, and let that peace overtake me. I need to make it a habit, dear Father, to find my peace in you.

O God, our help in ages past,
Our hope for years to come,
Our shelter from the stormy blast,
And our eternal home.

—Isaac Watts, "O God, Our Help in Ages Past"

My Creator, blessed is your presence. For you and
you alone give me power to walk through dark valleys
into the light again. You and you alone give me hope
when there seems no end to my suffering. You and
you alone give me peace when the noise of my life
overwhelms me. I ask that you give this same power,
hope, and peace to all who know discouragement, that
they, too, may be emboldened and renewed by your
everlasting love. Amen.

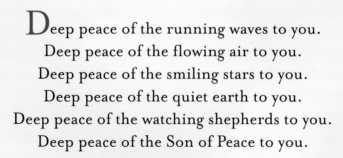

Deep peace of the running waves to you.
Deep peace of the flowing air to you.
Deep peace of the smiling stars to you.
Deep peace of the quiet earth to you.
Deep peace of the watching shepherds to you.
Deep peace of the Son of Peace to you.

—GAELIC PRAYER

Yes, Father in heaven, often have we found that
the world cannot give us peace, O but make us
feel that thou art able to give us peace; let us know
the truth of thy promise: that the whole world
may not be able to take away thy peace.

—SØREN KIERKEGAARD

A heart at peace gives life to the body.

—PROVERBS 14:30 NIV

*Dear God, I long to feel the peace you bring, the
peace that passes all understanding. Fill my entire
being with the light of your love, your grace, and your
everlasting mercy. Be the soft place that I might fall
upon to find the rest and renewal I seek. Amen.*

CHAPTER 3

The Blessings and the Lessons

Every good and perfect gift is from above, coming down from the Father of the heavenly lights, who does not change like shifting shadows.

—JAMES 1:17 NIV

God, it sometimes seems as though life is a big, giant classroom, filled with lessons that need to be learned. I ask that I be given the strength and courage to be up to the challenge of taking on each lesson as it comes. Let me learn from it so I don't have to repeat it. Even during the roughest of moments, help me understand that I am being blessed by the stress, so that I may pass each test with more wisdom, love, and faith in my heart.

Life is a series of tests, some harder than others. But we are always given exactly what we need to pass with flying colors if we trust in God.

So do not fear, for I am with you; do not be dismayed, for I am your God. I will strengthen you and help you; I will uphold you with my righteous right hand.

—Isaiah 41:10 NIV

*Counting our blessings isn't just about counting all
the good things that happen, but the bad things as
well. For often the greatest lessons happen only when
we are pushed to our limits and made to walk through
the fire. In the fire we are cleansed, purified, and
made stronger. We are stretched beyond our limits
and expanded into something greater than we
were before. Everything that happens to us offers
us a powerful opportunity to grow and become a
better person.*

A few years' experience will convince
us that those things which at the time
they happened we regarded as our
greatest misfortunes have proved
our greatest blessings.

—GEORGE MASON

When upon life's billows
you are tempest tossed,
When you are discouraged,
thinking all is lost,
Count your many blessings,
name them one by one,
And it will surprise you
what the Lord hath done.

—JOHNSON OATMAN JR.,
"COUNT YOUR BLESSINGS"

**And my God will fully satisfy every need of yours
according to his riches in glory in Christ Jesus.**

—PHILIPPIANS 4:19

The sun is a blessing. The storm is a blessing.
One brings warmth. The other brings
nourishment. Both are necessary for growth.

All that I am, Lord, is a result of all that you have given me. I am blessed beyond measure, in the miracles and the messes of each and every day. I welcome with open arms each new experience you bring into my life, knowing that it all balances out and that without the bad I would never feel the sheer joy of the good. With faith, courage, and hope, I face each morning with a resounding willingness to let life unfold as it will, and as you will it. I weather the storms and look afterward for the rainbows, knowing they all are a part of my wonderful life. Thank you, Lord.

Be strong and of good courage, do not fear nor be afraid of them; for the Lord your God, He is the One who goes with you. He will not leave you nor forsake you.

—DEUTERONOMY 31:6 NKJV

Blessed are those who know they are blessed when they are blessed! Too many people fail to notice the smaller miracles that occur each day, from the flowering of a plant outside their window to the lovely pattern the clouds make in the sky. So focused are they on the big miracles, the obvious and undeniable events and signs, that they ignore the more simple and subtle signs of God's love and mercy that appear along the way. Blessed are those who stop and smell the roses and who take time to notice the roses in the first place. Blessed are those who see the beauty in everything.

All of life's wonders are contained in the biggest
and the smallest of things. You can find the
miracle of life in the wide expanse of sky and in a
single blade of grass, if you have the eyes to see.

God, these problems you've placed before me are about to break me. I am not sure I can handle the stress and strain. I ask for your love, strength, and guidance to help me navigate these storms and find the sturdy ground beneath my feet again. I know that I am being challenged for a reason and that I will come away from this a better person, but it's during the dark and lonely nights and anxious, worry-filled days that I need someone to carry me. Help me, God, to find the way through and learn what I am meant to learn from this situation. Show me the blessings, God, in these lessons you are trying to teach me. Guide me toward the best outcome and solution for all involved. Amen.

I think in every lesson there's a blessing,
and there's so many blessings from all the lessons
I've had to go through in life.

—ALONZO MOURNING

**And the peace of God, which surpasses all under-
standing, will guard your hearts and your minds
in Christ Jesus.**

—PHILIPPIANS 4:7

*How much do I have left to learn, God, before
I can rest and relax? I feel like every day brings a
new problem to be solved, lesson to be mastered, or*

situation to be dealt with. I often feel I can't catch
my breath! But I do admit that each time I solve a
new problem, master a new lesson, or deal with a
new situation, I feel more confident, more grown up,
and more capable. I know I won't stop complaining,
God, and I know you won't stop delivering the daily
lessons, but thank you from the bottom of my heart for
giving me the clarity to see how blessed I am each time
I overcome my fears and move forward in faith. I get
this thing called life, even if it is harder at times than
I'd like it to be.

No testing has overtaken you that is not common to everyone. God is faithful, and he will not let you be tested beyond your strength, but with the testing he will also provide the way out so that you may be able to endure it.

—1 CORINTHIANS 10:13

As I look around and count my blessings, I am surprised by how many things in my life came to me through trials and tribulations. People, objects, and experiences I once wished would go away, that vexed and angered me, even caused me great pain, are now miracles I would never imagine doing without. Yes, good things have come my way in a positive fashion, but I really appreciate all that has come to me in times of darkness and despair. I see the good now in everything and how it has all fit together to make my life complete and whole.

Consider it pure joy, my brothers and sisters, whenever you face trials of many kinds, because you know that the testing of your faith produces perseverance. Let perseverance finish its work so that you may be mature and complete, not lacking anything.

—JAMES 1:2–4 NIV

Father in heaven, look down upon me today with love and mercy. I'm going through some tough times lately, and right now I fail to see the light at the end

of the tunnel. God, help me stay focused on the good that will come out of this, even if I cannot imagine what that good is at the moment. I have faith that you will always help me handle whatever situation I find myself in and that what you give me has a purpose for my life. But just for now, send a little bit of light my way to guide me through the long, dark night ahead. Amen.

Keep your face to the sunshine
and you cannot see the shadows.

—HELEN KELLER

But those who hope in the Lord will renew their strength. They will soar on wings like eagles; they will run and not grow weary, they will walk and not be faint.

—ISAIAH 40:31 NIV

Every person that comes into your life has a gift to give you. Even the people who push your buttons, make you angry, drive you crazy, and make you wish you had never met them have a lesson to teach you. And until you learn that lesson, God will send other people just like them into your life. How easy it is to love and care about your friends and family and those who support you. Yet even the people who seem to be your enemies deserve your love, your care, and your gratitude. Sometimes blessings come in the strangest of disguises.

Blessed are my enemies, for they have
as much to teach me as my friends.

**Bless those who persecute you;
bless and do not curse.**

—ROMANS 12:14 NKJV

*L*ord, as I lay down to sleep
tonight, I let go of the events of the
day, knowing that I did the best I
could, learned what I needed to
learn, and reacted from the highest
place possible. If I made mistakes,
I accept that and ask for the strength
and wisdom to do better tomorrow. If I hurt someone,
I ask for forgiveness, for it was not my intention. If I
didn't think before I spoke, or spoke out of turn, I ask
for more patience the next time around. I let go of it
all, knowing that each new day is a new opportunity to
take what I've learned the day before and start fresh.
I can and will do better tomorrow, Lord. Amen.

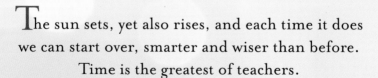

The sun sets, yet also rises, and each time it does we can start over, smarter and wiser than before. Time is the greatest of teachers.

Do your best to present yourself to God as one approved by him, a worker who has no need to be ashamed, rightly explaining the word of truth.

—2 TIMOTHY 2:15

Everyone always tells us to let go of the past, to take the lessons of yesterday and learn from them today. It is hard to do, letting go of the past, because in many ways we have unfinished and unresolved issues that still tug at our hearts and haunt our minds. But as long as we understand that it all happened for a reason, as part of God's bigger plan, we can more easily let go of the regrets and "what ifs" and "should haves" and come to a peaceful acceptance of what is. Then we can move on from there, equipped with the lessons and knowledge and wisdom that come from experiencing both the good and the bad.

Let go, let God, and let it be. There is no better way to live than by those three simple rules.

I remember going to school as a child and loving certain classes. The subject matter thrilled me, and the lessons were easy because I was excited to learn. Then there were classes I enjoyed less, struggled with, and eventually passed, which were harder to get through because my heart wasn't in them. And yet, I see that those difficult classes taught me so many important things that I didn't learn from the classes I enjoyed. I see now that the challenging classes helped shape me just as much and in ways I had no idea were possible at the time. Life is a series of fun classes and tough lessons, and those who strive to get good grades in both are truly blessed.

Blessed is the one who perseveres under trial because, having stood the test, that person will receive the crown of life that the Lord has promised to those who love him.

—JAMES 1:12 NIV

Blessed are those, dear Lord, who see the good in everything, who turn every negative into a positive, and who help others around them do the same. I ask to

be a person like that, a bright and shining light to those I love and to everyone I meet. I pray for guidance and wisdom so that I can serve as an example of someone who finds the glass half full—never half empty—and who learns from the trials of life. I thank you, Lord, for those very trials, for they have made me who I am today, and without them I would not be able to be of any service to those around me. For all that you have made me, and for all that you have asked me to live through, I am grateful. Amen.

Recognizing that we can always look at life from a different perspective is the way to find inner peace and happiness. Every cloud truly does have a silver lining if you look for it.

*G*od, may today be filled with more happiness than pain, with more peace than chaos, with more good than bad. May the sun shine a little bit warmer, and the night fall a little less cold, and may the new dawn be filled with more birdsong than tears. May I be a little stronger and a little less afraid. May I react with a little more love and a little less anger, and may I acquire a little bit more understanding and a little less intolerance. I know that life is made up of both dark and light, but I ask that the light always be brighter than the dark, and that I am always equipped with the courage, faith, and hope to make each day better than the day before. Amen.

Sometimes the greatest progress comes from the smallest of steps, as long as those steps are consistently taken in faith.

I will make them and the places surrounding my hill a blessing. I will send down showers in season; there will be showers of blessing.

—EZEKIEL 34:26 NIV

Today I pray not just for blessings, but for the ability to see them when they come disguised as obstacles and unanswered prayers. God, I know you don't always give me what I ask for, despite what I believe I need. It always turns out that had I gotten what I asked for, I would have ended up unhappy in ways I couldn't envision at the time. Your will is higher than mine,

*God, and your vision for me is clearer. I pray for
that same discernment when asking for blessings and
praying for miracles. I pray that what you give me,
God, is always best for me whether I like it or not at
the time. Amen.*

Learning a lesson may often hurt in the short
run, but in the long run, we are better for what
we have learned and experienced.

An unanswered prayer may at first seem like punishment, or as if God is withholding love from us, when in fact we are being loved and protected. God's "No" is often the doorway that opens to a wonderful "Yes."

We turn to God for help when our foundations are shaking, only to learn that it is God who is shaking them.

—CHARLES C. WEST

I love it when a friend is excited about something that just happened. "Chances are," she'll proclaim, "it's the best thing that will ever happen to me." And in that moment it truly is. But I love it even more when a friend recognizes the blessings in "the worst thing that ever happened to me," and comes out of a long,

dark journey through a challenging life experience with newfound resilience, strength, and faith. I love it when it happens to me also, because so often I've failed to be grateful for the dark part of the journey, in favor of the light. In the end, when we look back at the bigger picture, it appears that everything we go through is "the best thing that ever happened."

Seeing the best in the worst is
the highest form of wisdom and faith.

**But the wisdom from above is first pure, then
peaceable, gentle, willing to yield, full of mercy
and good fruits, without a trace of partiality
or hypocrisy.**

—JAMES 3:17

There's so much to be grateful for in this life!
Thank you, God, for your many blessings.

*All our opportunities, abilities, and resources come
from God. They are given to us to hold in sacred
trust for him. Cooperating with God will permit us
to generously pass on to others some of the many
blessings from his rich storehouse.*

Faith is the root of all blessings. Believe
and you shall be saved; believe and you will
be satisfied; believe, and you cannot but
be comforted and happy.

—JEREMY TAYLOR

Gratitude is an attitude of loving what you have, and this undoubtedly leads to having even more. When you open your eyes to the bountiful blessings already in your life, you realize just how abundant the world really is. Suddenly, you feel more giving, more loving, and more open to even greater blessings. Gratitude is a key that unlocks the door to treasures you already have, and it yields greater treasures yet to be discovered.

G od's peace among people
brings many blessings.

**Happy are the people to whom such blessings fall;
happy are the people whose God is the Lord.**

—Psalm 144:15

Change is never easy, dear Lord, but the blessings it bestows upon us are magnificent. Just ask the caterpillar struggling within the tight confines of a cocoon. Even as it struggles, it is becoming something glorious, something beautiful, soon to emerge as a winged butterfly. Change may bring temporary pain and discomfort, but it also brings the promise of a new life filled with joy and freedom and the ability to soar

even higher than we ever did before. Thank you for
change, God. Amen.

Lord, it's hard to count your blessings when all
around you is chaos and despair. Though my heart is
heavy and my mind cluttered, please help me realize
that before a flower shows its beauty to the sun, it is
first a seed buried in the dirt. Help me stand above the
negative things in life and cast my eyes instead upon
the positives that are always there, like the seedling,
growing toward the moment when it will appear above
ground, facing the sun.

Lift up your heart in sweet surrender to the
God who is waiting to shower you with blessings.
Lift up your soul on wings of joy to the God who
is waiting to guide you from the chaos of shadows
out into the light of a peace that knows no equal.

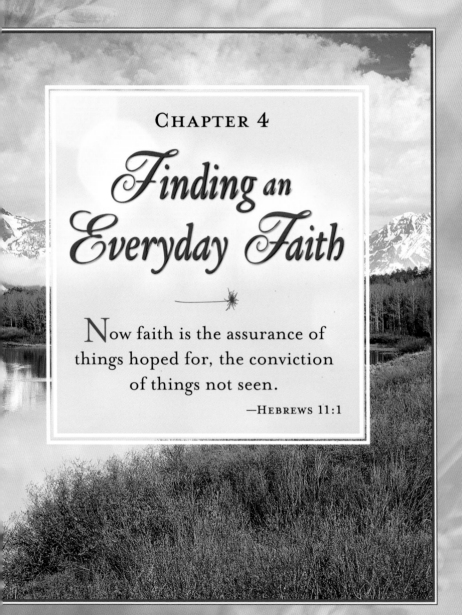

CHAPTER 4

Finding an Everyday Faith

Now faith is the assurance of
things hoped for, the conviction
of things not seen.

—Hebrews 11:1

Dear Lord, give me a faith that lasts longer than my fear. It's easy to feel strong and good when all is well, but when everything around me seems to be a huge mess, it's hard to keep the hope alive. With your loving presence, I know I will be able to weather each daily storm, believing that I have the inner and outer resources to do so. I know, dear Lord, that you never give us more than we can handle, but perhaps just for today can you pass a little more faith my way?

We may wake up to stormy skies, but faith is what we hold onto until the sun breaks through the clouds again.

Have faith in God. Truly I tell you, if you say to this mountain, "Be taken up and thrown into the sea," and if you do not doubt in your heart, but believe that what you say will come to pass, it will be done for you. So I tell you, whatever you ask for in prayer, believe that you have received it, and it will be yours.

—MARK 11:22–24

Faith is knowing that even if we cannot see something, it is there anyway. Faith is a kind of certainty in an unseen power that loves us and wants the best for us. Faith is believing in miracles even if a miracle seems to be nowhere in sight. Faith is letting go of control, knowing that God controls everything for us. All we have to do is suit up and show up and keep moving forward. Just waking up in the morning requires faith, for we have no idea what

each day will bring. But upon waking, and hearing the birdsong, and feeling the sun's warmth, we set aside our fears and move forward.

Faith is taking the first step even when
you don't see the whole staircase.

—MARTIN LUTHER KING JR.

People who have done great things often say that
their greatest resource and power came from a deep
and abiding faith: faith in a power greater than
themselves, faith in humanity, and faith in themselves.
The ability to keep going toward a desired purpose or
goal, even when it seemed utterly impossible to reach,
is what makes these individuals stand out and achieve.
We all have the opportunity to find that faith within
and bring it forth so that we can succeed at whatever
it is we desire, whatever our purpose may be. Faith is
not something given only to the lucky few. Faith is a
blessing we are all born with.

He replied, "Because you have so little faith. Truly I tell you, if you have faith as small as a mustard seed, you can say to this mountain, 'Move from here to there,' and it will move. Nothing will be impossible for you."

—Matthew 17:20 NIV

God, grant me the faith to be my best today. Though the children are calling and the work is pressing upon me, and the coffee is not made and the phone is ringing, and the pets are asking to be fed and the house is a mess . . . give me the faith today to stand up to it all with grace and even a bit of humor. Without my daily dose of faith, life can get a little overwhelming, and on some days, a lot overwhelming. Just a little bit of faith with my coffee is enough to start off the day with the resourcefulness, strength, and wisdom I need to make it through in one piece until bedtime. Amen.

A daily dose of faith is like vitamins
for the body, mind, and spirit.

"*To them that have, more shall be given.*" I am certain this was about faith, and about how those who have faith are given more in life. There is a door leading to miracles, but the key to that door is faith, along with the belief that the world is a friendly place and that we are loved and cared for by a God who wants the best for us. Without faith, we cannot enter the kingdom that is beyond that door; with faith, we cannot only enter the kingdom but also partake of all the blessings and wonders within its walls.

Though we do not know what lies beyond
an open door, faith allows us to walk through
it anyway and experience the miracles
that exist only when we overcome fear and
doubt and "just go for it."

*Looking back on all those times when I was younger,
when I thought things would never get better or I was
in the midst of heartbreak over the loss of a love or
a job or a dream, I remember always having a sense
of something pulling at me to keep on going. No
matter how hard the road ahead seemed, I felt
something tugging me forward, even if I had no idea
where I was going to end up. I realize now that it was
faith urging me onward, faith calling me to believe
that things would improve. And the funny thing is,
they did.*

The little voice within that whispers to keep on going when the going gets tough is the voice of faith. Listen to it, for it will never lead you astray.

Have mercy on me, O God, have mercy on me, for in you I take refuge. I will take refuge in the shadow of your wings until the disaster has passed. I cry out to God Most High, to God, who vindicates me. He sends from heaven and saves me, rebuking those who hotly pursue me—God sends forth his love and his faithfulness.

—Psalm 57:1–3 NIV

Father in heaven, I ask that you instill in me a strong and abiding faith to help me through my day. No matter what challenges I face, no matter what drama people throw my way or what obstacles I have

to get around, give me a steadfast certainty that I will prevail. Give me a faith that will move mountains, though more likely I will only need to move molehills. Give me a faith for this day that stretches out before me, filled with promise and possibility. Amen.

With faith as your constant companion,
the road of life is much easier to travel,
even when detours and dead ends appear
along the way. Faith goes before us,
making clear and right our way.

*Why is it so hard, dear God, to have faith
and trust that all will be well? I have faith
that the sun will set each night and trust it will
rise in the morning. I have faith that gravity
will hold me to the earth and trust that what
goes up will come down. I have faith that my
bills will arrive on time, that the mail will
come each day, and that the lights will go on when I
flip the switch. Yet when it comes to having faith that I
will never be let down or abandoned, God, and having
trust in you to always watch over me, I often falter.*

Help me have the same strong faith in the unseen things as I have in the things I can see, and help me trust that your will, God, is always higher than mine. Amen.

All who call on God in true faith, earnestly from the heart, will certainly be heard, and will receive what they have asked and desired.

—MARTIN LUTHER

In this you rejoice, even if now for a little while you have had to suffer various trials, so that the genuineness of your faith— being more precious than gold that, though perishable, is tested by fire—may be found to result in praise and glory and honor when Jesus Christ is revealed.

—1 PETER 1:6–7

Faith is to the mind as love is to the heart. Faith eases a mind overwhelmed by the hows and the whys of a situation. Faith brings peace to the chaotic thoughts, worries, and anxieties. Faith is a soothing balm to the racing mind filled with fear. Faith is a comforting blanket to the mind gone cold with doubt and negativity. Faith empowers a weak mind that does not believe it can overcome a challenge and emboldens a meek mind that is afraid to step out of its comfort zone. Faith is a friend and an ally and a warrior for the mind that knows that sometimes the answers to life's questions lay beyond the limitations of reason.

When thought and action alone are not enough to face an obstacle or overcome a challenge, call upon the warrior known as faith. For only faith can go where the rational mind cannot and see what the reasoning mind fails to see.

*L*ord, let my faith be a light to guide my way today. Whether skies are sunny or stormy, let me move according to my faith, secure in the knowledge that it will lead me to the path that is right and true. Let me leave all control to you, Lord, and follow the beacon of light that is my faith in you, the way the boats at sea follow the lighthouse beacon to the safety of shore. Let me stand in faith today, no matter how hard the winds blow. Let my faith take root like those of a redwood tree, strong and firm.

Faith is the "yes" to every "no" and the "can"
to every "cannot." Faith gives us the power
to stand against anything and prevail, even
when we don't know how we will do so. Faith
requires no knowledge of how it works, just
the acceptance that it does work.

**For the Lord loves the just and will not forsake his
faithful ones.**

—PSALM 37:28 NIV

When there seems to be no way out, faith provides a way in. When all doors have been closed, faith opens up a window. When our challenges threaten to drown us, faith offers us a lifeboat and guides us back to shore. The walls of life can sometimes close in on us, leaving us feeling small and weak and powerless, but faith takes us by the hand and walks with us until we feel big and strong and powerful again.

Examine yourselves to see whether you are living in the faith.

—2 CORINTHIANS 13:5

"You gotta have faith," goes the famous pop song, and I am blessed, dear God, with plenty of faith in your presence and power in my life. I am also blessed with friends and family I can rely on, as well as my own good company. My faith is strong and true, for it has never ceased to provide me with the courage, wisdom, and guidance I need to be patient and at

peace even when things around me are a mess. Thank you, God, for building in me a foundation of trust and faith that everything happens for a reason and that I am always loved, cared for, and protected, even when it appears to the contrary. For I know now that faith speaks of a power far greater than appearances and far stronger than effects. Faith knows no boundaries. Amen.

Whe all else fails, have faith! It costs nothing more than the willingness to surrender control and give up the need to be Master of the Universe. Let God run the ship. Your job is to enjoy the ride.

We are always confident . . . for we walk by faith, not by sight.

—2 Corinthians 5:6–7

One of the hardest roles a woman plays is that of a mother. Mothers are expected to handle any obstacle, weather any storm, and navigate any conflict and do it with patience, love, and grace. As a mother, I know how hard this can be and how much it requires sheer faith that my best will always have to be good enough.

Without faith in God and in my own abilities, I would never be able to care for others and for myself without falling apart! Faith is a mother's best friend and constant ally. We moms may not always be able to fix every boo-boo, but with faith we know we can, at the very least, ease the pain.

I don't pray for God to take my problems away,
I pray only for God to give me the strength
to go through them.

—JOSE LOZANO

Nature is filled with examples of faith in action. Go out on a cloudy and cold day. Behind those clouds is a vast expanse of blue sky and a sun that warms the soul. Look up at the moon hanging in the night sky. That moon rises and falls like clockwork. The bird knows where to fly, and the flowers bloom right on schedule. The animals live, the trees grow tall, the insects hum and buzz, and not one of them worries about tomorrow. The sun does not fret with anxiety about whether it is rising correctly. The horse does not get insecure when it gallops. Everything in nature runs on the faith that all is well and perfect just the way it is.

Only people lack faith in the natural order of creation. Worry not, for God's plan is always at work and always working perfectly.

**If you do not stand firm in faith,
you shall not stand at all.**

—ISAIAH 7:9

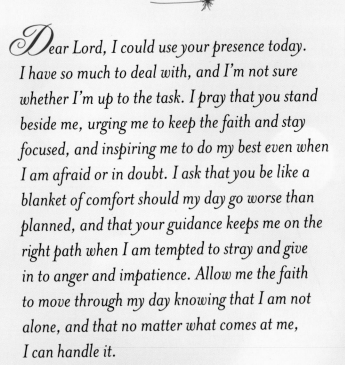

*Dear Lord, I could use your presence today.
I have so much to deal with, and I'm not sure
whether I'm up to the task. I pray that you stand
beside me, urging me to keep the faith and stay
focused, and inspiring me to do my best even when
I am afraid or in doubt. I ask that you be like a
blanket of comfort should my day go worse than
planned, and that your guidance keeps me on the
right path when I am tempted to stray and give
in to anger and impatience. Allow me the faith
to move through my day knowing that I am not
alone, and that no matter what comes at me,
I can handle it.*

We may not always feel like we are up to the task,
but our faith will make certain we rise
to the occasion when we have to.

So then faith cometh by hearing, and hearing by the word of God.

—ROMANS 10:17 KJV

People will let me down and disappoint me, the car won't always start, and the check won't always arrive on time, but my faith in you, God, never fails me. Like a steadfast and eternal flame, faith burns brightly within, helping me overcome the disappointments of daily life and finding peace when it would be so much easier to just give up and give in. I know, God, that I can always rely on you to be there, and that when others fail to come through, you never turn your back on me. Without faith, life would be a scary place. But with faith, I can face each fear as it comes my way, with trust and confidence that you are bigger than my fears. Thank you, God.

With faith as our weapon, we can face down any monster that fear puts in our path and move forward with boldness and confidence.

I pray that out of his glorious riches he may strengthen you with power through his Spirit in your inner being, so that Christ may dwell in your hearts through faith.

—EPHESIANS 3:16–17 NIV

I pray for three things today: a faith that never falters, a hope that never fails, and a courage that never weakens. Material blessings are wonderful, but with these three things I truly feel that I have the kingdom of heaven at my feet, with all it contains. Faith, hope, and courage are like food, water, and air and bring me sustenance and vitality, especially on those days when I feel weak and hopeless and not up to the challenge of anything. I pray today for just these three things, God, knowing that you will always supply my every need. Faith, hope, and courage—the most important blessings of all. Amen.

Money can buy us so many wonderful things, but it cannot buy us the best things, for those are free to us and in constant supply when we put our faith in God.

Be joyful in hope, patient in affliction, faithful in prayer.

—ROMANS 12:12 NIV

Some of our biggest challenges come in the form of other people. They frustrate us, upset us, anger us, and sometimes make us crazy. Often we lose our patience and even our love for them. This is where faith comes in. When we trust that every person we meet is doing the best they can with what they have, and that there is a reason for all of them to be in our lives, including those who most push our buttons, we realize that all we need to do is treat them with kindness, forgiveness, and compassion. We just need to have faith that everyone we know counts, even the ones we wish we'd never met!

Faith is the glue that keeps relationships together, even when they are difficult and we cannot see their worth. Everyone in our lives is important to our growth in some way. We just need to have faith that one day that importance will be revealed.

Those who have faith are blessed along with Abraham, the man of faith.

—GALATIANS 3:9 NIV

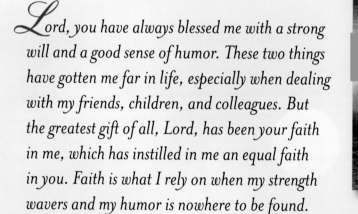

Lord, you have always blessed me with a strong will and a good sense of humor. These two things have gotten me far in life, especially when dealing with my friends, children, and colleagues. But the greatest gift of all, Lord, has been your faith in me, which has instilled in me an equal faith in you. Faith is what I rely on when my strength wavers and my humor is nowhere to be found. Faith is my go-to power to get through each day and night, and then do it all over again. Faith is my up-and-at-'em when I feel more down-and-out. I thank you, Lord, for the amazing grace of your presence in my life and for this unshakable faith of mine! Amen.

Faith is what keeps you smiling through the pain,
laughing through the fear, and dancing
through the rainstorms of life.

Faith requires personal commitment,
decision, and purpose. God sets the plan,
but we must do the legwork.

Faith is proven through neither logic nor
reason; it must be felt with the heart.

Let love and faithfulness never leave you; bind them around your neck, write them on the tablet of your heart.

—Proverbs 3:3 NIV

Father, there are many events over which we have no control. We do have a choice, however, to endure trying times or to give up. The secret of survival is remembering that our hope is in your fairness, goodness, and justice. When we put our trust in you, we can remain faithful. Our trust and faithfulness produce the endurance that sees us through the tough times we face. Please help us remember that. Amen.

Faith in God's love frees me to be the real me, for I remember that God sees me as I am and loves me with all his heart.

In [Christ] and through faith in [Christ] we may approach God with freedom and confidence.

—Ephesians 3:12 NIV

Lord, give me the faith to take the next step, even when I don't know what lies ahead. Give me the assurance that even if I stumble and fall, you'll pick me up and put me back on the path. And give me the confidence that, even if I lose faith, you will never lose me.

[Jesus said,] "Very truly I tell you, whoever believes in me . . . will do even greater things."

—John 14:12 NIV

Each prayer is a message of faith in God. We are saying, "I trust you; lead me. I believe in you; guide me. I need you; show me." When we offer ourselves openly, he will always answer.

Faith and fear cannot coexist. One always gives way to the other. It is necessary for us to be constantly building up our faith to overcome the numerous sources of destructive disbelief all around us. We need to be continually working at rekindling the gift of God that is in us, which is our faith in him and in his promises. We must be dedicated to developing a spirit of love and power and discipline within ourselves. Studying the words of the scriptures, meditating on them, keeping God's commandments, and praying daily are some of the ways we can keep our faith strong day by day. By focusing on these things, we shut out fear and cultivate faith.

Take up the shield of faith, with which you can extinguish all the flaming arrows of the evil one.

—Ephesians 6:16 NIV

Lord, give me hope,
Give me patience to cope
And a reason to keep on trying.
Take my trembling hand
Give me power to stand
And a faith that is strong and undying.

Faith is more than a passive idea; it is a principle that motivates our day-to-day decisions and actions. Would the farmer plant if he did not expect to harvest? Would the student read and study if she did not believe it would improve the quality of her life? Would we work hard each day if we did not hope that by doing so we might accomplish something worthwhile? We act daily upon things we believe in, though we cannot yet see the end result. This is the faith we live by, whether we identify it as such or not.

Faith is for that which lies on the other side
of reason. Faith is what makes life bearable,
with all its tragedies and ambiguities
and sudden, startling joys.

—MADELEINE L'ENGLE

[Jesus said,] "I have prayed for you . . . that your
faith may not fail."

—LUKE 22:32 NIV

You cannot control every circumstance,
but you can respond to each one in faith.

—ELLIS MORRISON

CHAPTER 5

God's Help in Tough Times

And we know that all things work together for good to those who love God, to those who are the called according to His purpose.

—ROMANS 8:28 NKJV

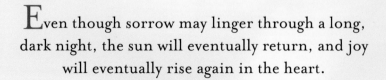

Even though sorrow may linger through a long, dark night, the sun will eventually return, and joy will eventually rise again in the heart.

*H*eavenly Father, if you weren't here for me, I don't know what would have become of me during my most difficult times. I know that more difficulty may lie ahead, but like the psalmist said, "I will fear no evil, for you are with me." It's not that I don't feel the pain or grief—you know I do—but it doesn't destroy me. Thank you for the times you've held me through the darkness and given me comfort and strength to go on. Thank you, too, for the hope that remains with me, leads me forward, and helps me heal.

For I consider that the sufferings of this present time are not worthy to be compared with the glory which shall be revealed in us.

—ROMANS 8:18 NKJV

*L*ord, *when physical limitations begin to press in,
I don't want to be defined by any loss of health I'm
experiencing, whether it's a temporary impairment
or something more permanent. I realize that
this body won't last forever—that it is indeed
wearing out. And while I hope to be as whole
as possible for as long as possible, you gave me
this body, and so I will be grateful for every
day of life you give me in it. When there is
pain, give me grace to endure it. When there is
frustration, carry me in your patience. When
there is sorrow, comfort me with reminders of
my future with you. And with every physical
loss, let there be a spiritual gain that outweighs
it and makes it seem small in comparison.*

"Don't ever stop 'walking your faith.' Place
your life and your case in God's hands, then rest!
If you lose hope and faith, you lose two of the
essential ingredients in the healing process."

—TESTIMONIAL OF UNIDENTIFIED MAN IN *TRIUMPH
THROUGH TRAGEDY*, DAVID WILKERSON

The wisdom of this world points to a home, a job, a retirement, insurance benefits, and such as the source of security, Father. But I've been reflecting on this value system and realizing how precariously perched are people who put their trust in such things. I know there is nothing wrong with any of these, and they are blessings. But Lord, you are my source of security. All of the things that money can buy in this world can be swept away in a moment, and if my faith is in those things to keep me safe or to make me secure, I am going to find myself at a loss. But you never fail, you are rock solid, you are my safety and security in this life and my certainty for life beyond this one. Thank you.

No matter what I may lose in this life,
there is never any risk of losing what is
ultimately important when my spiritual
life is fully vested in God.

**What, then, shall we say in response to these
things? If God is for us, who can be against us?**

—Romans 8:31 NIV

*Father, you've created a wonderful gift to humanity
on the earth by giving us the animal kingdom, and
especially pets we adopt and nurture and come to love
as family members. But when we lose one of them,
it's more painful to say good-bye than we like to
admit. After all, these are friends that have loved us
unconditionally and have trusted us so fully to take
care of them. Their vulnerability is moving, and when*

they leave us, we grieve. Before when we grieved,
they comforted us. Now that they're gone, the sorrow
is compounded in their absence. We're sometimes
afraid to make too much of it to others who may not
understand, but with you there is no such fear. You
gave them to us, knowing we would love them but
eventually lose them, and so we look to you as our
source of comfort when we grieve their passing.

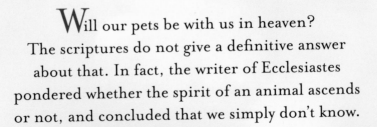

Will our pets be with us in heaven?
The scriptures do not give a definitive answer
about that. In fact, the writer of Ecclesiastes
pondered whether the spirit of an animal ascends
or not, and concluded that we simply don't know.
Still, we have reason to hope that we'll see our
favorite animal friends again.

How do I say good-bye to someone I've loved so much in this life, Father? To let them go, to live life with that empty spot where they once were feels so awkward and unnatural. It seems wrong to carry on without them. Something inside me shouts, "As if I could!" And yet I must, and I do, and it's so difficult. How do I find "normal" now in those places where we always stood together? Please help me. Carry me and grant me quiet healing that happens as grief takes its course. And please, even in this grief, let me find joy in the memories of our time together on this earth.

The Lord is close to the brokenhearted and saves those who are crushed in spirit.

—PSALM 34:18 NIV

Father, you have said that those who wait for you will never be ashamed for having put their trust in you. So I call out to you in my distress, knowing that you hear me. As I pray and trust and wait for your merciful intervention—I know your timing is perfect but so often different than what I think it should be—to support me and hold me steady as you have so many times in the past.

Answer me when I call to you, my righteous God. Give me relief from my distress; have mercy on me and hear my prayer.

—Psalm 4:1 NIV

*W*hy is there evil in the world? Why do bad things happen to good people? I hate these horrible things that plague our existence! Why don't you stamp out the pain and sorrow once and for all, Lord? What are you waiting for? Ah, Lord! I know evil was introduced into the world through a willful act against your truth and love. And since then it just keeps going on and getting worse. I also know that you have a plan to put an end to it all, but that you are patient as you wait for people who are estranged from you to return. Help me be an ambassador of your truth and love, to carry your light everywhere at all times, even where darkness seems to be prevailing.

All the world is full of suffering.
It is also full of overcoming.

—HELEN KELLER

**Call on me in the day of trouble;
I will deliver you, and you shall glorify me.**

—PSALM 50:15

———————✳

*O*ur minds search for reasons, Father.
They grasp and grope and grapple to
discover why. Yet tragedy doesn't send
a card with its condolences or a letter
of explanation as to why we are the
ones it has visited. It just comes and
overshadows our lives, takes things
from us, turns our reality upside down.
Sometimes it strikes quickly, leaving
us numbed and trembling, while other
times it seems to hang on like a bulldog,
inflicting pain upon pain. I just don't
understand this. I know in time some
answers may emerge. But right now I need you to
shelter me from the anger and frustration and fear
and doubt that rise up within me. I know you are not
afraid of my struggle. You understand and you care.
But I am afraid of losing my faith in your goodness
and love for me. Hold me close, Father.

The biblical character Job brings an empathic word to those who suffer. His voice speaks to us even today as we sense his anguish and yet see his devotion to the God of his life. Consider journeying through Job and finding some comfort as you bring your suffering alongside his.

**And the God of all grace, who called you to his
eternal glory in Christ, after you have suffered a
little while, will himself restore you and make you
strong, firm and steadfast.**

—1 Peter 5:10 NIV

*I don't know how much longer you will grant me
life, Father. Our journey here is just that—a journey*

with a beginning and an end. We don't get to see
our beginning in the sense of remembering it. But
sometimes we see our end as it approaches. Then those
vague thoughts about what comes next come into sharp
focus. We take stock of our journey—what has and
hasn't been done or said or accomplished. We prepare,
we mourn, we say good-bye. There is one thing that
doesn't change, though—one thing that is sweet and
constant along the path of life: the assurance of your
love and of the eternal home with you that you have
prepared for those who love you. Help me, even in the
valley of the shadow of death, to keep that reality in
view with eyes of steadfast faith.

Even as the reality of death closes in, the bright
reality of eternal life opens up wide before our
hope, as faith turns its face fully heavenward.

*L*ord, losing a loved one to a destructive path is almost like a death! The person we love seems to disappear, and we struggle to find ways to show this person love without supporting the things that are destroying them. It's such a helpless feeling to watch a

*loved one self-destruct. I pray for the person on my
mind right now who is going the wrong way. I ask you
to intervene, to show me how to love them best even if
they misunderstand that love, and to keep them safe
as you work in their situation to draw them into your
saving grace.*

The people who wander into darkness often
have a sense of being "too bad" to ever be
accepted back into God's grace. When we assure
them of our unconditional love, while still
holding them to the truth, it can help them
glimpse God's own heart of love for them.

**But you, Lord, are a shield around me,
my glory, the One who lifts my head high.
I call out to the Lord,
and he answers me from his holy mountain.**

—PSALM 3:3–4 NIV

God will not permit any troubles to come upon us, unless He has a specific plan by which great blessing can come out of the difficulty.

—PETER MARSHALL

I'm convinced that my life is not a series of random events. I believe, Father, that you are working all things together for good purposes in my life as I trust in you. And I know that includes the long, dark valleys as well as the mountaintop experiences. Of course I can always see that more clearly in retrospect, but I have learned, too, to trust that this is the case even when I am in the middle of something painful and distressing.

God is a great listener and encourager. David and Job complained to God in their misery, but they always "landed on their feet" when they were done, finding God to be the comfort they needed.

*P*lease forgive me when I complain, Lord. I don't mean to ignore the things that are good in my life— and there are many. But pain and struggle and weariness shout so loudly that sometimes they're all I hear. When I need to cry, let me cry on your shoulder where I know I'll be heard and understood, consoled

*and encouraged. Other people might minimize what
I'm going through or rant about things I can't control.
Neither is helpful in moving me toward a better place.
But when I pour out my discouragement to you, I
know that you'll listen and then gently turn my heart
back toward what brings strength and grace to carry
on. You even make me able to give thanks and rejoice
in you. Thank you for lifting me up.*

The people who are looking on, Lord, who see my suffering and how I respond to it . . . do they see how much I rely on you? Do they know that you are the one who is carrying me through? I could not make it without you. I would crumble. Please give me opportunities to tell just how much you mean to me and how your grace has seen me through everything. I want others to know that you will be there for them when they struggle. I want them to understand that they can look to you and find all the help they need.

But we have this treasure in clay jars, so that it may be made clear that this extraordinary power belongs to God and does not come from us. We are afflicted in every way, but not crushed; perplexed, but not driven to despair; persecuted, but not forsaken; struck down, but not destroyed.

—2 Corinthians 4:7–9

Losing a baby . . . it's such a deep grief in a woman's life, Father. It's one of the most difficult things to accept, and it makes it hard to trust that you are still there, that you still care. Sometimes there is shame involved, often anger, and always an ache that just doesn't go away. How can you understand my pain—

this grief so specific to a woman? How can you know what I'm going through? I want your comfort, but since you are the author and sustainer of life, it's hard not to feel like you're opposing me! . . . Ah, how gently you remind me. You too were bereaved of a beloved child. That is how you know. And because of what you sacrificed for me, I have assurance that I will see my child again. Please, Father, see me through this grief.

But we do not want you to be uninformed, brothers and sisters, about those who have died, so that you may not grieve as others do who have no hope. For since we believe that Jesus died and rose again, even so, through Jesus, God will bring with him those who have died.

—1 Thessalonians 4:13–14

The news is filled with tragic events, Lord: wars, natural disasters, accidents, deaths, and all of the other disturbing things that take place at home and around the world. How do I reconcile all of this with your message of hope? How do I encourage people who feel overwhelmed by all the darkness that seems to deepen with each passing generation? Help me be both gentle and bold in telling people about your light of truth and love that overcomes darkness. Let them see that you prevail not only in individual lives and

communities of faith that honor and worship you,
but also that you promise a place to come where
darkness will no longer exist to trouble us.

Hope anchored in God's promises is a
certainty awaiting its fulfillment.

Father, right now in the middle of this trial, I feel my need for rest. Please grant me the sleep I need. May your Spirit quiet my mind and still my heart when I lie down, and let it chase away any distressing dreams. Let your word fill my thoughts so that as I drift off to sleep I am surrounded by assurances of your watchful care over me. Thank you, Father, for the rest you bring even when life is at its most difficult.

I lie down and sleep; I wake again, because the Lord sustains me.

—PSALM 3:5 NIV

I remember someone saying that what doesn't make us bitter will make us better. Lord, I've never seen the good in becoming bitter about life. Your grace is always big enough for each of us, whether our trials are few or many. I want to become better, though, when I come through a painful struggle, a difficulty, or a loss. Help me remember that the work of making me better is your work. My work is to remain faithful to you—trusting in you. From within that place of trust, you will fashion a better kind of faith, hope, and love within me.

We are always in the forge, or on the anvil; by trials God is shaping us for higher things.

—HENRY WARD BEECHER

I am holding on to your promises, Lord, in these trying times. You never fail, so I know I can count on everything you have said. If there are times when I feel you haven't kept your word, it surely means I have narrowed your meaning to some expectation I have, rather than waiting to see in what way you will make good on your word. Grant me patience as I wait. I will wait for you.

The scriptures are full of calls and commands to be patient while God is at work. With each reminder there is a promised reward for those who choose to wait. Don't give up!

*H*elp me resist the temptation to try to escape this struggle by means of things that are not good for me, Lord. There are substances in this world that can temporarily numb pain but that also threaten to steal years of my life. Grant me help and wisdom in what I choose along this painful path. Help me to be honest and accountable to those around me. I feel my vulnerability right now, so I look to you to keep me safe from harm.

For whatever was written in former days was written for our instruction, so that by steadfastness and by the encouragement of the scriptures we might have hope.

—ROMANS 15:4

Father, there is a prayer I once heard that is attributed to fishermen: "O God! The sea is so wide, and my boat is so small." I feel like that tiny vessel on the great sea today. This pain is too big for me; I am too small to bear it. But you are bigger than this ocean of sadness I feel, and my small strength is supported by your great love for me. I feel adrift, but you are guiding me to shore by your gentle currents. I will trust you.

Like the sun, the greatness of God's tender mercies toward you may be obscured by clouds of pain, but like the sun, God's love is there—it is always there.

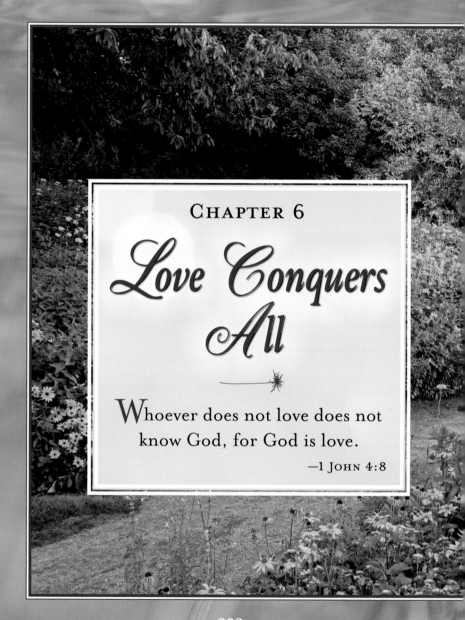

CHAPTER 6

Love Conquers All

Whoever does not love does not know God, for God is love.

—1 John 4:8

God in heaven, I pray to you today not to ask for material things. Instead I ask for only one thing: your steadfast love. With your love in my life, all else will come to me, a showering of blessings and miracles big and small. Love is the gate to abundance, and your presence, God, is the key that opens the gate to all that fills the soul and quenches the spirit. I pray today for love, that I may receive it as well as give it, and that it may open my heart to ever-increasing joy and happiness. Amen.

Love is a force more formidable than any other. It is invisible—it cannot be seen or measured, yet it is powerful enough to transform you in a moment, and offer you more joy than any material possession could.

—BARBARA DE ANGELIS

*O*ne of love's greatest expressions comes in the form of other people. Our friends, families, and colleagues all manifest God's love on earth, making us feel less alone and more accepted, understood, and cared for. The people we are blessed with, even those who sometimes get on our nerves and push our buttons, are sent from on high to keep us company as we walk the road of life. Love is best expressed from one heart to another, and both hearts benefit from the joy and the power of that exchange.

Beloved, let us love one another, for love is from God, and whoever loves has been born of God and knows God.

—1 John 4:7

The gift of love comes not only from receiving it but also from giving it. So many lonely souls in the world need kindness and compassion: let us be a blessing of love to all we meet today. So many people are hurting and afraid: let us shower kindness and love on everyone we encounter, for we never know when one simple act of kindness may turn a life around. Love is a gift that can be shared over and over, and it never runs out. Love replenishes itself, renews itself, and is ever-present. Give the gift of love freely, knowing that it makes the world a better place and will return to you in the form of love, like a perfect circle, ever turning.

No one has ever seen God; but if we love one another, God lives in us and his love is made complete in us.

—1 John 4:12 NIV

What if we all could put the same amount of time and effort into giving love to others as we put into picking out and giving birthday gifts? Love costs nothing, takes little time, and is worth more than its weight in material things.

Lord, it's easy to love my family and friends, but I am having a hard time figuring out how to love my enemies. Some are like emotional vampires, with the drama and the complaining. Some only come around when they want or need something. I know that everyone is a child of God, but sometimes I wish I could play on a different playground! Help me, Lord, to find the patience, tolerance, and kindness to turn the other cheek and love the hardest to love as well as the easiest. I know everyone deserves my compassion, but I am not always up to giving it. Amen.

Be kind to unkind people.
They probably need kindness the most.

—AMISH PROVERB

You have heard that it was said, "You shall love your neighbor and hate your enemy." But I say to you, Love your enemies and pray for those who persecute you, so that you may be sons of your Father who is in heaven. For he makes his sun rise on the evil and on the good, and sends rain on the righteous and on the unrighteous.

—Matthew 5:43–45

One of the greatest lessons we can ever learn is to love ourselves. Then and only then do we seem to be able to truly love others. Without first recognizing our own worth and how very much God has given us his blessings and love, it is impossible to feel that same sense of worth and deserving toward others. We cannot give what we don't have inside. So when it comes to love, often the best place to find our soul mate is within our very own soul. Fall in love with yourself, then loving others will be easy and natural

*and genuine, without conditions and rules and
jealousies that come from a lack of self-respect and
confidence. It all begins within.*

Love begins within our own hearts,
where we realize just how cherished we are
by the one who made us. From there,
we can go forth and love the world.

God, show me how to love unconditionally, without expectation of reciprocation or return. Show me how to love those who seem unlovable, and teach me to see in them what you see. Show me how to reach out to others in love but also how to receive love, because I often fail to love myself or let others love me. Show me how to use the energy of love to make my life, and the lives of everyone around me, brighter and happier. Show me how to love, God, the way you love me. Amen.

Someday, after mastering the winds,
the waves, the tides and gravity, we shall harness
for God the energies of love, and then,
for a second time in the history of the world,
man will have discovered fire.

—PIERRE TEILHARD DE CHARDIN

And above all things have fervent love for one another, for "love will cover a multitude of sins."

—1 PETER 4:8 NKJV

Only love can transcend time and space and reach across vast horizons to touch those who are so far away, bringing them hope and comfort. Love is a thing, and an energy, and an action, all at once. Love goes where fear cannot tread and dares to walk where even faith loses its footing. Love knows no beginning and has no end, because when one experiences love, it is outside the confines of the clock—eternal, enduring, and everlasting.

Time is too slow for those who wait,
too swift for those who fear,
too long for those who grieve,
too short for those who rejoice,
but for those who love, time is eternity.

—HENRY VAN DYKE

A mother's love is the strongest force known to humankind. Neither fire nor wind nor the oceans' mightiest waves can compare to the love a mother has for her children. When a mother's child is sick or in danger, a mother becomes a warrior queen, equipped with a power unlike any other—the power of love. She can comfort and heal and teach and guide. She will sacrifice and give until it hurts. She will never stop loving her child. Thank you, God, for a love so fierce and mighty. And thank you for your love, which gives us the power to love others.

The bond between a mother and her child
is made of pure and unconditional love
mixed with courage, strength, compassion,
and good old-fashioned wisdom.

I often see an elderly couple walking along the streets of my neighborhood, hand in hand. They don't always talk, they just walk, enjoying the evening air and being in each other's company. How blessed it is to find someone special to spend your life with, someone to love and to be loved by who is more than a spouse, but also a partner, a companion, a friend. Love that lasts seems so rare these days, but it does exist and we all deserve to find it. Love that lasts isn't flashy and nonstop fun and games. It is the ability to live out each day with another human being, the small and boring stuff included, and to know that you are never alone because there is always one special person who is willing to walk with you, hand in hand.

Let love be genuine; hate what is evil, hold fast to what is good.

—ROMANS 12:9

The truest expression of love is the ability to be one's real self with another person. Love asks not for flashy and expensive gifts, but for the gift of authentic presence in another's company. Love allows each person to be who they are alone, together.

God above, is there someone out there made just for me? I am ready to love and to be loved by someone special, but the dating pool seems to have dried up. Send me a good man to love and cherish, to be my friend and life mate and partner in joy. Guide me to the perfect mate, one who matches and complements me, yet challenges me and keeps me growing and wanting to be a better person. I know he is out there and that you have chosen him carefully for me. If you feel I am ready to meet him, God, please send him my way. Amen.

God would not have made us with
such big and loving hearts if he did not intend
us to share them with others.

There is no better medicine to the
ills and injuries of life than love.

*L*ove *makes all things possible. Love heals the deepest of wounds. Whenever life presents us with situations and events that frighten us and test our limits, love is what takes us beyond the boundaries of what we thought we could withstand. The power of love sustains us in times when our hearts and souls hunger for something to hold onto, and love holds us up when the ground beneath us begins to shift. Love makes all things possible.*

God is not unjust; he will not forget your work and the love you have shown him as you have helped his people and continue to help them.

—Hebrews 6:10 NIV

Thank you, God, for good friends! We all get by with a little help from those special people God has chosen to bless us with. Whether they are old friends from school days or new friends we just made, friends are the juice of life. We can be ourselves with our friends, let our hair down, and let it all hang out. We can share our fears, our hopes, our dreams, and our sorrows with friends and feel listened to, understood, and supported. Friends are like gemstones, precious and rare.

Life is so much more enjoyable with the love of good friends to sustain us, support us, inspire us, and cheer us on through good days and bad.

Dear God, teach me to act with love today. I know my words are not enough; show me how to behave and act in loving ways toward everyone I meet. I've always believed that actions speak louder than words, but I often fail to walk my talk. I pray for the will to always walk with integrity, honesty, and authenticity, doing unto others as I would have them do unto me. Help me remember the Golden Rule of love—to give what I would like given to me, not just in words but also in deeds. Amen.

Dear children, let us not love with words or speech
but with actions and in truth.

—1 JOHN 3:18 NIV

Lord, why do we expect so much from those we love? Why is it that we always hurt the ones we love the most? Perhaps it is this thing called expectation, which tells us that when we love someone, they owe us something in return. Help me today, Lord, to love without expectation. I know love is not truly love if it asks for something in return, like a bargain or a debt. Teach me to love others the way you love me, Lord, without chains or conditions or rules and regulations. Thank you, Lord.

Love is always bestowed as a gift—
freely, willingly and without expectation.
We don't love to be loved; we love to love.

—Leo Buscaglia

Love is not reserved just for the two-legged beings in our lives, but also for our four-legged friends. A pet can be the perfect example of unconditional love, giving to us everything it has and asking so little in return. Our beloved creatures become a part of our family, and we experience joy when they are happy and such deep grief when they pass on. Nothing is quite like the excitement a pet has for us when we come home from work or school. All they ask of us is our time and a little bit of attention, and they readily give us their hearts. If only people could love without reservation the way our pets love us.

God could not be everywhere so he made
pets to keep us company, enrich our lives,
and remind us what real unconditional love is.
Our pets are angels with paws and tails
and whiskers and fins for wings.

Father in heaven, there are so many lonely people in the world, longing for someone who will love and care for and understand them. I am one of those lonely people, God, who wants to find someone special to live out my days with. Please bless me with a love that is true and honest and real, a love that will endure all of life's ups and downs and still stays strong, a love that is devoted and faithful and uplifting. My heart is open and ready to give of itself and to receive the love of someone who is also open and ready to give. Guide me to the one you have chosen for me, God, I ask of you today in prayer. Amen.

No love is more powerful, inspiring, and enduring than the love between two people who have decided to give of themselves without fear or doubt. Two hearts unite and become even stronger as one in love.

I love my family and friends for the way they make my days brighter, my nights warmer, my challenges easier, and my fears smaller. I love them for the laughter they provide when I need it most, and for the shoulders to lean on when I cry. I love them for the times they try my patience as well as the times they are my biggest cheerleaders, because they always have my best interests at heart. I love them for being there with a heart full of comfort when I hurt and for knowing when I need to be alone. I love them for being them and allowing me to be me.

To love him with all your heart, with all your understanding and with all your strength, and to love your neighbor as yourself is more important than all burnt offerings and sacrifices.

—Mark 12:33 NIV

Even though we must walk our life path alone, we can spend part of that journey with others who love us and want nothing more than our company along the way. These are the people we call our family, our friends—our home.

I pray for a way, dear Lord, to love the uncertainty of life. I pray for the courage and faith to love how little control I have and how often things change just as I am getting used to them. I pray, Lord, to love life's ebbs and flows and to be at peace with the cycles of the wheel that turns whether I want it to or not. It's easy to love my life when all is going well and I am excited and happy, but it's not so easy to love it during the down swings and low times. Help me, dear Lord, to love all of it, each day, as it comes. Amen.

Resisting life's situations leads to sadness, hopelessness, and a sense that nothing has a purpose. Trust life and let it unfold as it will, knowing that a loving God is in control and knows what is best for us.

Just as a newborn infant needs a loving touch to thrive and grow, we need to be loved as adults. Without love, we wither and fade. Love does not have to be big and bold, it can be the care of a friend, the hug of a colleague, or the joy a pet has for us when we walk through the door. To know that we are in some way important to others, and that we matter, is a form of love that helps us thrive and expand and grow so we can begin to feel more loving toward others in return. We are loved by God and by those we dare to reach out to each day, even in the smallest of ways. No act of kindness goes unnoticed.

Asimple kindness or a gentle touch is all
it takes to make someone realize they are cared
for. Love is not a big, complex gesture but a
whisper that says, "You matter to me."

I give you a new commandment, that you love one
another. Just as I have loved you, you also should
love one another.

—JOHN 13:34

*L*ife is a love song, lived in words, deeds, and experiences. How much life gives back to us depends on how much love we put into it. So make the life you live a love-filled celebration of gratitude. Be thankful not just for the good things but also the bad, for they have all shaped you into who you are now. They have gotten you to where you are in the present. Take your past and learn from it, then leave it behind. Let the future unfold in its own time. Remember, life is a love song, meant to be sung in order from verse to chorus to the next verse. You would not sing a song out of order, would you? Then why would you live your life that way?

Just the fact that we are here, alive, on this glorious planet, is proof that we are loved beyond measure by a God who created us to go forth and share the joy of what we have been blessed with.

CHAPTER 7

A Healing Power

Heal me, O Lord, and I shall
be healed; save me, and I shall be
saved; for you are my praise.

—JEREMIAH 17:14

Dear God, I am praying today for the healing of someone I care deeply about. I know that everything happens for a reason, but I ask that you help my loved one get through this challenging illness. May your mercy and grace shine down upon my friend, providing courage and comfort and a sense of being deeply cared for. May your light provide warmth and strength through each coming trial, for there will be many. Heal my loved one today, God. Amen.

When someone we love is ill, we can turn to God in prayer and healing. God's love heals all ills and overcomes all obstacles.

God, I think about all the people in the world today
who are hungry, alone, afraid, and dying. I see how
blessed my own life has been, and I ask today for
healing love for those who are far less fortunate than
I am. I have so much, and many have so little. I want

to share my blessings and my care. Guide me toward a path that will help provide healing to others, no matter who they are or where they've been in life. Everyone deserves to be happy, healthy, and at peace. Dear God, I pray today for a global healing. Amen.

An outstretched hand toward those in pain becomes a merciful extension of God's healing touch.

Praise the Lord, my soul, and forget not all his benefits—who forgives all your sins and heals all your diseases, who redeems your life from the pit and crowns you with love and compassion.

—PSALM 103:2–4 NIV

Healing comes in many forms. We can have a healing of our bodies, but also of our hearts, our minds, and our spirits. Sickness and disease sometimes attack the nonphysical parts of us, leaving us feeling tired, alone, and ready to give up on life. But the same power of healing that can cure a body of disease

can cure the rest of us. From a broken heart to a withered spirit, beaten down by the challenges and disappointments of life, we can find healing in the love of friends, family, and God.

The Lord protects and preserves them—they are counted among the blessed in the land—he does not give them over to the desire of their foes. The Lord sustains them on their sickbed and restores them from their bed of illness.

—PSALM 41:2–3 NIV

The road of life is a journey of woundings and hurts, healings and lessons. Just when we seem to be traveling along at an easy pace, life will throw an obstacle in our path that makes us long for the good ol' days. Time, then, steps in to help us slowly heal, giving us renewed strength and increased wisdom to carry along with us as we head further down our path. Eventually, the painful lessons become fewer and farther between, as we learn how to reach deep within for the healing we need when problems arise. We start to walk in faith, confidence, and trust, knowing that we are loved and cared for by a loving God every step of the way.

God allows time to help us heal the
wounds of the past, and in the healing, we are
given the gifts of wisdom and experience
to take with us into the future.

*Dear Father in heaven, I realize this illness will be
taking me back to you soon. But I am still praying for
healing, this time for my spirit and my soul. I know
that not all healing is physical, that your healing touch
can still be on me. Give me confidence that my faith
has not been weak, and that is not why I am dying.
Your ways are not known to me, and I have to rely on
you. Ready my spirit to meet you, Lord. And please
be with my family and loved ones after I leave; keep
your hands on their hearts. Thank you, dearest Father.
Amen.*

Indeed we count them blessed who endure. You have heard of the perseverance of Job and seen the end intended by the Lord—that the Lord is very compassionate and merciful.

—James 5:11 NKJV

*G*od, help my family, for I, the queen of the household, the mom, am feeling icky today. Teach them to feed themselves, get dressed for school and work, and do all the things I would be pushing them to do on a normal day. Guide them to the right drawers, closets, and cubbies to find the things I usually find for

them. *Help them help themselves, and maybe help me
a little, too. Rarely do I take the time to relax and get
well when I am ill, because if I am sick for too long,
the whole house unravels! I pray for a fast healing,
but not before my family has learned to take care of
themselves, and maybe even offer me a little TLC.
Come to think of it, maybe I'll just lay here in bed for
a day or two—I need the rest! Thank you, God, for
renewed health. Amen.*

A happy, healthy
home and family
starts with a happy,
healthy mom who
is in touch with her
healing God!

The wounds of the heart are often the hardest to heal. When a loved one passes on or we suffer the heartbreak of a love that was not meant to last, we are left with an emptiness and a sense of despair that make us feel powerless. To others, we seem fine on the outside, but we are crying on the inside. To heal the wounds of the heart, we must first grieve the loss and not resist the tears. Only through feeling our grief can we begin the process of moving forward with life again. The heart will mend once it heals, and this may take some time. We may always remember the pain, but we will be stronger for having experienced it.

Loss requires a special kind of healing
that only time and tender, loving care can
provide. The heart is strong and resilient
and will be open to love again.

Father above, thank you with all my heart for the amazing healing you have blessed me with. I was lost and afraid, struggling with my illness, sure it would get the best of me. But through my faith in you and your steadfast love, I am now free from disease and on my way to a complete recovery. Thank you, Father, for giving me a second chance to know what life is like in a body that is strong and resilient and filled with vitality. You have brought light into the dark places and returned me to wholeness, and for that I am forever grateful. Amen.

Be gracious to me, O Lord, for I am in distress; my eye wastes away from grief, my soul and body also.

—Psalm 31:9

When we pray for healing, our prayers will be heard, and if it is your will, God, our bodies will be whole again.

Having a child with a chronic illness or condition can break even the strongest parent's heart. We want the best for our children, and that includes a life that is free from pain and suffering. But often God's will has another purpose for what our children experience, and we must dig deeply for the faith and the trust to accept that will. We can pray for healing and do all we can for our children, but their outcome is in the hands of a higher power that loves them and sees for them what we cannot see. As hard as it is to do, we must let go and let God take over and know that his love for all his children is eternal, steadfast, and true.

Then they cried to the Lord in their trouble, and he saved them from their distress; he sent out his word and healed them, and delivered them from destruction. Let them thank the Lord for his steadfast love, for his wonderful works to humankind.

—PSALM 107:19–21

Lord, I can rail against this illness and be angry, but the truth is that we all are given challenges and battles, and this one is mine. Instead of being angry, I pray instead to you, dear Lord, for the strength to overcome what I am being asked to deal with. I know that I am no more special than anyone else and that I must deal with the rain as well as the sun, the pain and suffering as well as the joy, just like everyone else. I am not asking that you remove these trials from me, but only that you make me capable and courageous enough to withstand them. Amen.

The call of God involves earthly suffering because through it we may magnify His power to keep us and demonstrate His grace in our weakness. Earthly suffering, bravely borne, shows powerfully the reality of the living God.

—STUART BRISCOE

$\mathcal{T}$he amazing thing about becoming ill—whether with something as difficult to deal with as cancer or a heart attack or just a lousy week's worth of stomach flu— is how grateful people feel once they've healed and

overcome the illness. So many people tell such inspiring stories of getting the terrifying diagnosis of an awful disease, only to find the strength and will to survive that they never knew they had. So many come out the other side to later claim that the disease was a blessing in disguise, giving them the opportunity to become better human beings and appreciate life more than ever before. Healing can be more than just recovering. It can be empowering.

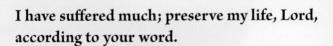

I have suffered much; preserve my life, Lord, according to your word.

—Psalm 119:107 NIV

Lord, shine your love down upon me today and make me whole again. I've suffered a lot these past few months and I know it was all in your hands, but I could use some rest and healing. I've always been strong and able to handle what I needed to handle, but I know I still need the tender, loving care only your presence in my life can provide. Keep me in your loving arms today, Lord, as I rise and face another set of challenges. I know together we can get through this and that in the end your will be done. Amen.

Healing requires patience and the understanding that divine timing may not be the same as our own. God knows best what to do . . . and when.

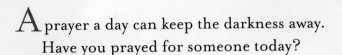

The power of prayer is the power of loving and compassionate words and thoughts to bring healing. God hears our prayers and sets into motion what is needed for healing to take place. Our role is to continue to send the love out to those who need it, whether it be to ourselves or our loved ones or even the world in general, because everyone is suffering. Everyone could use some prayer, a little love, and a little compassion. Pray for someone today who may not be doing well, and let your own light reach out and brighten the darkness that surrounds them.

A prayer a day can keep the darkness away. Have you prayed for someone today?

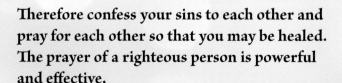

Therefore confess your sins to each other and pray for each other so that you may be healed. The prayer of a righteous person is powerful and effective.

—JAMES 5:16 NIV

God, someone I love has passed on today, and I pray now for healing for the family and friends left behind. Though one soul is at peace, so many more now grieve and suffer the pain of having to say good-bye. Though our loved one is gone from us physically, we know that the spirit is eternal. But help us in our mourning today, and bring comfort to all of us who remain with heavy hearts. Thank you, God.

The loss of a loved one requires a deep healing that is part faith, part trust, and part understanding. We may not understand why someone has to die, but we know it is a part of life and that we who stay behind must continue to live.

When a healing appears in your life, it's as if the clouds have parted to let the warm, bright sunshine through again. Everything takes on a joyful glow, even the mundane things you rarely noticed before, because you are seeing with a new sense of wholeness. The world appears more friendly, and everyone you come in contact with is precious as you realize the fragility of life. No moment goes wasted again, for now you understand the gift of the present and the gift of God's healing presence. A healed mind, body, and spirit bring into sharp focus all the blessings in life.

Then your light will break forth like the dawn, and your healing will quickly appear; then your righteousness will go before you, and the glory of the Lord will be your rear guard.

—Isaiah 58:8

In my hour of need, I turn my eyes inward
to a place where God's strength flows like a river
of healing waters. I immerse myself in
the current, and I am renewed.

Glory to you, God, for bringing comfort to those
who call upon you in prayer. Your compassion and
grace bless those who ask for strength and courage
through the toughest of times, and your joyful presence
is like a soothing balm for those who have overcome
a great challenge and now seek rest. Today I celebrate
the return to wellness that you have brought into my
life and the healing that has made me able to stand up
and face each day with a smile on my face. I happily
and gratefully look forward to the future with a
newfound sense of faith and the desire to share my
story of healing with those who need it. May I be
a blessing to them today. Amen.

One of the greatest blessings that accompanies a healing is the ability to go forth and tell our story to others who may be going through similar challenges. Our triumph may be just what they need to hear about to restore their own faith.

When we are in perfect health, we take it for granted and expect it to last forever... until we are stricken with disease or injury. Then we long to return to the times when we were stronger, more vital, and more alive. Good health is not just about getting sick and being healed, it's about staying well as much as we can, in body, in mind, and in soul. Yes, we may have times when we become the victims of a bug, a disease, or even something far more serious, but during the days when we experience wellness, we must be grateful and live in the moment and enjoy it while it lasts.

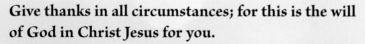

Give thanks in all circumstances; for this is the will of God in Christ Jesus for you.

—1 THESSALONIANS 5:18

Dear Father in heaven, tonight I lay down to sleep with a heavy heart and a mind filled with anxiety and concern. Tomorrow I will have surgery and I am afraid, not just for myself, but also for my family, who depend on me to be up and about and whole and healthy. I ask tonight that you watch over me during this procedure and that you bring me out of it with no problems or obstacles. I ask that you provide the love, strength, and fortitude I will need in the coming weeks to recover and heal and be my old self again soon. Thank you, Father. Amen.

Most of us will, at some point in our lives, face a huge health issue or challenge. We already have what it takes to overcome any illness, but just in case, God will be watching over us, like a physician on high whose shift never ends.

God, send me an army of angels today that I can dispatch to all the friends and loved ones who are currently going through health challenges. From cancer to lupus to a broken leg and the flu, it seems everyone around me is in need of some loving care and healing. If you'd like me to, God, I ask that you empower me with the ability to take my love and compassion and help them in any way I can. Let my prayers go before me, preparing those people for a wave of healing love that comes from my heart directly to theirs. I may not be an army of angels, but I will do what I can as a friend and a loved one to help those who need me today. Amen.

We don't have to be an angel, a doctor, or even a trained nurse to offer some tender loving care and healing to those who are suffering. All we have to do is show up and show how much we love them.

Let each of you look out not only for his own interests, but also for the interests of others.

—PHILIPPIANS 2:4 NKJV

To a child, a hug can heal a boo-boo, as can loving words and a gentle touch. To an adult, a bowl of hot soup takes care of a cold and a shoulder to cry on strengthens a broken heart. No matter who we are or how old, we want to know that others care, especially when life isn't going so well. No gesture is too small to have an impact, and no kindness will go unnoticed.

The simplest acts of compassion go a long, long way for a body that aches, a spirit that grieves, and a soul that seeks joy amidst despair and darkness. All are ingredients in the recipe for healing.

In the softest of touches and the gentlest of gestures there is powerful healing energy that can help restore a broken body, spirit, and heart to wholeness.

Is anyone among you in trouble? Let them pray.
Is anyone happy? Let them sing songs of praise. Is
anyone among you sick? Let them call the elders of
the church to pray over them and anoint them with
oil in the name of the Lord. And the prayer offered
in faith will make the sick person well; the Lord will
raise them up.

—JAMES 5:13–15

Lord, heal the earth and all its living things today, of disease and war, violence and death, poverty and destruction. Help each of us find our own way to heal our little corner of the planet and to spread a love that impacts everything in its path. If enough of us pray, we can move mountains and calm storms. If enough of us take action, we can save our planet and eradicate suffering in every corner of the world. Teach us, Lord, to be good stewards of this amazing earth we live on, and may we treat all its creatures as precious gifts you have bestowed upon us. Amen.

There is so much need all over the planet for healing, it can sometimes seem overwhelming and hopeless. But just praying and doing our small part can have a snowball effect, especially when combined with the prayers and efforts of others. One day, we will wake up to a better world.

CHAPTER 8

God's Soothing Comfort

The Lord himself goes before you and will be with you; he will never leave you nor forsake you. Do not be afraid; do not be discouraged.

—DEUTERONOMY 31:8 NIV

People have told me, Father, that being alone does not have to mean feeling lonely. But I'm feeling lonely today. I could use some human companionship, but maybe this is a time for me to learn to draw near to you as my comforter and friend. Help me discover true contentment with you in these alone times, and as you see fit, please bring along the people you know will give the kind of comfort and encouragement I need.

Are we weak and heavy laden,
Cumbered with a load of care?
Precious Savior, still our refuge—
Take it to the Lord in prayer.
Do thy friends despise, forsake thee?
Take it to the Lord in prayer;
In His arms He'll take and shield thee,
Thou wilt find a solace there.

—JOSEPH SCRIVEN, "WHAT A FRIEND WE HAVE IN JESUS"

*P*lease help me Lord; I feel abandoned! I wasn't ready to keep moving forward on my own. I want to trust in you for what lies ahead, but I cannot even imagine how to do that. Faith means trusting that you're with me and will see me through, even when I cannot see the outcome. I'm taking a deep breath, and—despite the pain I feel—I'm going to keep on going, one step at a time, as I trust you to show me how to live again. Thank you for being here with me.

**Cast your cares on the Lord and he will sustain you;
he will never let the righteous be shaken.**

—Psalm 55:22

When the psalmist wrote his famous shepherd song, he gave a single reason why he did not fear evil (e.g., hardship, difficulty, abandonment, the wicked treatment of others). He said because you are with me, Lord, I won't be afraid. He certainly felt the pain of rejection and abandonment by his surrogate father, Saul, but he found his comfort in fellowship with the Lord, whom he characterized as a caring shepherd.

The Lord is my shepherd, I lack nothing. He makes me lie down in green pastures, he leads me beside quiet waters, he refreshes my soul. He guides me along the right paths for his name's sake.

—PSALM 23:1–3 NIV

Someone else has taken the place I used to fill, Lord. I used to be the one responsible for making sure certain things got taken care of. Now I feel displaced, and I miss my work and my sense of belonging. You must have other work for me now, though. Help me focus on finding it and doing it as well as I've done my other work in the past. Help me let go of any bitterness in my heart and embrace the new roles and responsibilities you will put before me. I am yours, and I know you have good plans for me.

As painful as it may be, being displaced for a time can sometimes carry the blessing of disentangling our identity from things that are not us and reminding us who the essential person is within this skin we live and travel in.

The economy has left me without the job I am used to doing, Father. It feels so strange to be out of work. I know so many others are experiencing the same sort of thing, and there are those who are struggling even more than I am. Help me to be empathic and encouraging to the people I meet who are looking for work. Help them to see how I am able to trust in you and be at peace, even in difficult circumstances, because you, not a job, are my provider. I look to you to meet all my needs.

**Praise be to the ... Father of compassion and the
God of all comfort, who comforts us in all our
troubles, so that we can comfort those in any
trouble with the comfort we ourselves receive
from God.**

—2 Corinthians 1:3–4 NIV

Rejection is so painful and humiliating, Father. It makes me feel unwanted and valueless. Help me remember, though, that how others may or may not value me is not the same as how you value me, and your "valuing meter" is not broken or skewed like our human ones. As my Creator, you see all the potential you have built into me as a unique masterpiece of your own design. Keep me looking to you for my sense of value so that I will not become lost in the wilderness of others' opinions. Thank you for valuing me as you do, for loving and accepting me at all times.

There is great freedom and joy in seeing
ourselves through our Creator's clear eyes,
rather than through the eyes of others
like us who, as the apostle Paul put it,
"see but a poor reflection."

Remember your word to your servant, for you have given me hope. My comfort in my suffering is this: Your promise preserves my life.

—Psalm 119:49–50 NIV

*L*ord, your Word is at my fingertips any time I want to find comfort, help, hope, and strength. But often I get caught up in listening to what my friends have to offer in the way of support rather than looking to you as my primary source. The truth is, though, that other people's words are not the same as yours. Theirs are limited to what they know, to their experiences, even to their level of comfort in telling me the truth. Your Word, however, knows no such limitations. You are thoroughly true, unconditionally loving, and you are all knowing and all wise. You know me through and through, and your words are the words of life I need to heal and comfort my hurting soul.

*W*hen I'm tempted to withdraw from people, Father, help me check that impulse if it takes me beyond just temporary alone time. You have made me to be a part of the community of faith, to be a comfort to others in their times of need, and also to receive comfort from them in my own difficulties. Don't let me get away with playing "lone ranger." Keep reminding me that I'm part of a family—your family—and help me stay connected to the people you've put in my life to support and encourage me along my way.

Two are better than one, because they have a good
return for their labor: If either of them falls down,
one can help the other up. But pity anyone who falls
and has no one to help them up.

—ECCLESIASTES 4:9–10 NIV

*hank you for the comfort of a good friend, Father.
There have been times in my life when friendship
has helped me through what felt like an impossible*

passage. I'm feeling the need for the support of friends again right now, and I pray that in your wisdom and compassion you will open up the time and space for the right friend or friends to be available to talk and listen and be there as I press forward in this difficult part of my journey.

Just as you've been a faithful friend to others, your friends are counting on you to lean on them, as well.

Being able to trust you, dear Lord, brings me the greatest comfort of all. You are completely reliable and faithful—the one constant in my ever-changing reality. What would I do without your presence to comfort me along my way? There is no doubt I would be looking to people and things that cannot deliver what only your love can provide. I will be forever grateful that I've come to know you as my Savior and Friend.

Abide with me; fast falls the eventide;
The darkness deepens; Lord with me abide.
When other helpers fail and comforts flee,
Help of the helpless, O abide with me.

—HENRY F. LYTE, "ABIDE WITH ME"

**The Lord is a stronghold for the oppressed,
a stronghold in times of trouble.**

—PSALM 9:9

Father, as a friend's newborn got his first needle sticks after he was born, I had to leave the room because his cries were heartbreaking. But the blood had to be drawn to make sure he was okay. Later he will have immunizations that will also cause him temporary pain but will guard him against serious illness and disease. It made me think about some of the pain I experience in my life—the hurts and struggles and frustrations that I just don't understand. Surely your heart is moved when I cry out to you, but you also see down the road and know what I need to learn and how I need to grow. Hold me and comfort me when I don't understand, just as my friend held her baby close and soothed away his pain and fear.

There is nothing that moves a loving
father's soul quite like his child's cry.

—JONI EARECKSON TADA

*F*ather, I know that grieving is a process. It can't be rushed; it has to take its course. Sometimes I wonder, though, Will this never end? *Just when I think I'm moving forward, another unexpected wave of sorrow knocks me over. I am still off balance, so I will take this one day at a time with you beside me, with your promise of comfort to carry me. You have been my source of comfort from the start, and I know you will continue to console me until the waves of grief subside.*

Blessed are those who mourn, for they will be comforted.

—MATTHEW 5:4 NIV

I didn't know that a simple word of encouragement could bring such comfort, Father, until I felt my own need to be comforted. I don't mean the blithe cliché a well-meaning soul may utter to ease the awkwardness one feels in the face of another's pain. I mean the kind of encouragement that comes from the psalms of David or a note from a close friend or a warm hug with the words "I'm praying for you" whispered in the ear. Thank you for these tangible comforts from your heart and from the hearts of folks who truly understand.

Sometimes the most comforting words
are the fewest, carefully chosen from within
a heart of deep empathy.

I don't know how much longer this pain will engulf my heart, Lord. It feels as if it has come to stay. In fact, I can't imagine my days and nights without it, now that this sorrow has been visited on my life. My sadness is a strange thing—like a companion I don't want but don't know how to do without. Jesus, please bring your gentle light into this dark place and gradually let it increase until there is daylight in my soul again. I know that the tender beams of comfort with which you illuminate my way will in time guide me into the full light of joy again.

But I will sing of your strength, in the morning I will sing of your love; for you are my fortress, my refuge in times of trouble.

—PSALM 59:16 NIV

I'm going to keep coming to you, Father, for the comfort I need. When I spend time with you, my heart is calmed, and I know you are holding me. There is no other friend, support group, or counselor who can take your place. I'm thankful for those other sources, but your presence is my mainstay. My prayers will continue to be lifted up to you throughout this day and all the days of my life.

Prayer crowns God with the honor and glory due to His name, and God crowns prayer with assurance and comfort. The most praying souls are the most assured souls.

—THOMAS BROOKS

I feel so alone in this trial, Father . . . alone in the sense that there isn't another person on earth who can support me right now. Help me not lapse into self-pity or blame others for not being there for me. That won't help matters, I know. But the temptation is there, so help me look away from those things and look steadfastly to you and the comfort you are holding out to me. It is sufficient, and in fact it's far more than that: Yours is the best support and comfort there is. Even if there were multitudes of human supporters at my side, none of them could comfort and encourage my heart like you do. Thank you, Father, for being my truest friend.

To look to human sources for what only God can provide is to delay delivery of the essentials we so desperately need and he so willingly supplies.

*T*hank you for the gift of music, Father. Your Word
says there is music in heaven, and you have given it to
us here on earth as well. The power music has to touch
a soul is truly miraculous; it speaks the language of

deep emotion. Thank you for the strong comfort you give me through different kinds of praise and worship music—the effects of those melodies and lyrics help make your presence seem even nearer.

Sometimes a light surprises
the child of God who sings;
it is the Lord who rises
with healing in his wings.
When comforts are declining,
God grants the soul again
a season of clear shining,
to cheer it after rain.

—WILLIAM COWPER,
"SOMETIMES A LIGHT SURPRISES"

I need your comfort, Lord. I need to be reminded of your goodness, your faithfulness, your promises, and your power to carry me through today. When I feel lonely and abandoned, may your faithful voice remind me that I am not alone. When I feel lost, may your guiding presence lead me in the right path. When I forget to praise you, remind me of all I have to be thankful for. And when I need encouragement, cheer my heart with a glimpse of your goodness.

[Jesus said,] "But the Helper, the Holy Spirit, whom the Father will send in My name, He will teach you all things, and bring to your remembrance all things that I said to you."

—JOHN 14:26 NKJV

Father, thank you for the comfort of so many simple things: the sunshine, a cup of coffee or tea, the voice of a friend. There are things I take comfort in that I don't even think about. And each of these is a kindness from you. Help me see it that way and not take your gifts for granted. Your comfort is all around me if I will see it.

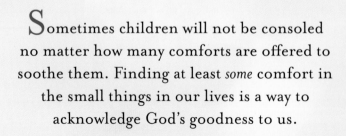

Sometimes children will not be consoled
no matter how many comforts are offered to
soothe them. Finding at least *some* comfort in
the small things in our lives is a way to
acknowledge God's goodness to us.

**He heals the brokenhearted,
and binds up their wounds.**

—Psalm 147:3

*Father, I need a hand, but I don't know who to turn
to. All my friends and family are too far away to help.
I feel isolated, and I'm not sure what to do. I want to
ask the people at church, but I don't want to impose
on them. They've always seemed willing to reach out
where there's a need, but I'm afraid to bring my need
out into the open. But I need the comfort and help of
your people right now. Please give me the courage to
open up to them and allow them to be your hands in
my life.*

One of life's great comforts when you choose to trust in God is the ready-made family you can find in his people wherever you may go.

Feeling adrift and alone is difficult. A soul wants to feel connected, anchored, Father. But even while I feel this isolation around my soul like a great wall, I have hope of something better still to come. That's why I don't feel despair. You keep assuring me that where I'm at right now is not permanent. And I believe you. Thank you for keeping my heart buoyant, my hope and faith alive. And thank you for the comforting assurance of something joyful ahead.

Hope fills the afflicted soul with such inward joy and consolation, that it can laugh while tears are in the eye, sigh and sing all in a breath; it is called "The rejoicing of hope."

—WILLIAM GURNALL

CHAPTER 9

Forgiving and Living

If we confess our sins, he is faithful
and just and will forgive us our sins and
purify us from all unrighteousness.

—1 JOHN 1:9 NIV

O Lord, your willingness to forgive is astounding!
You've never done anything wrong, and yet you are
ready to forgive those who have sinned against you
whenever they sincerely confess and turn away from
the wrong they've done. I want to thank you for being
so merciful toward me, for forgiving my debt of sin.
I will always praise you for your goodness in dealing
with me so gently. Help me remember to be merciful
toward others, just as you have been toward me.

The scriptures tell us that as far as the east is
from the west, that is how far God removes
our sin from us. Once God removes our sin,
it is gone. While we may remember it from
time to time, God chooses to forget it.

*S*ometimes I forget how much I've been forgiven
and how much I need ongoing forgiveness from you,
Father. I start looking at others and their issues and
get a self-righteous feather in my cap. How ridiculous
that must seem from where you stand! Thank you for
your patience with me. Forgive me for thoughts and
attitudes that have a superior tone. Fill me with the
humility of one who has been forgiven much and so
has learned how to love much.

Before we get all enamored with our high-and-mighty importance, it's a good idea to take a backward glance at the "hole of the pit" from which Christ lifted us. . . . It has a way of keeping us all on the same level—recipients of grace.

—CHARLES R. SWINDOLL, *GROWING STRONG IN THE SEASONS OF LIFE,* "NO PLACE FOR PRIDE"

For all have sinned and fall short of the glory of God.

—ROMANS 3:23 NKJV

*There are times when it's hard for me to believe
that you will forgive me again, Lord. Especially when
I keep stumbling over the exact same issue. I know
I get fed up with others who repeat the same mistakes.
I begin to think of you in terms of how I am, but you
are not like me. While you are no pushover, you are
also not one to hold a grudge when I am truly sorry
about my words, attitudes, or actions that are not
pleasing to you. You invite me to get right with you
again so that our fellowship can be restored, because
you value our relationship more than you value your
right to be vindicated. How much I have to learn
from your love!*

When we struggle with the need to forgive, we can ask ourselves: Is it more important for me to be right in this case and hold my ground or to forgive and restore the relationship?

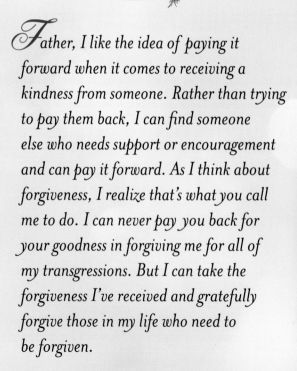

Father, I like the idea of paying it forward when it comes to receiving a kindness from someone. Rather than trying to pay them back, I can find someone else who needs support or encouragement and can pay it forward. As I think about forgiveness, I realize that's what you call me to do. I can never pay you back for your goodness in forgiving me for all of my transgressions. But I can take the forgiveness I've received and gratefully forgive those in my life who need to be forgiven.

Bear with one another and, if anyone has a complaint against another, forgive each other; just as the Lord has forgiven you, so you also must forgive.

—COLOSSIANS 3:13

Be kind and compassionate to one another, forgiving each other, just as in Christ God forgave you.

—Ephesians 4:32 NIV

I remember an account from your Word, Lord, in which one of your disciples asked how many times he should forgive someone when he was asked for forgiveness. When the disciple proposed what others considered a generous amount, you dwarfed his number by turning it into an exponent. Ah, Lord! Forgiveness is an ongoing need we have. And because we continually battle our selfishness, it will always be an ongoing need. But you are willing to keep wiping our slate clean, to keep encouraging and equipping us to grow into your ways. Thank you for your example. Help me joyfully embrace a lifestyle of forgiveness as I live in your freedom.

When someone asks for forgiveness,
we may hesitate, wondering if forgiving them is
tantamount to enabling them to continue
hurting us. But forgiveness can be extended
while we use tough love to draw needed
boundaries within the relationship,
which will encourage healthy change.

If your brother or sister sins against you, rebuke them; and if they repent, forgive them. Even if they sin against you seven times in a day and seven times come back to you saying "I repent," you must forgive them.

—LUKE 17:3–4 NIV

I've discovered an amazing irony, Lord. . . . I thought that when I forgave someone I was setting them free, but I've come to realize I'm the one who is freed when I forgive! The other person might still be tangled up in their own stuff, but when I forgive them for what they've done to harm or offend me, I'm no longer enslaved by resentment and anger. I'm even able to see that person through eyes of compassion, or at least have a heart of concern for them. Lord, if you hadn't called me to forgive others—if you hadn't forgiven me—I might never have gotten free in this way. Thank you.

My forgiving someone may or may not change them, but their response is not my responsibility. My responsibility is merely to forgive, and when I do, it changes *me*—transforms me, in fact, as I become more like Christ.

And forgive us our debts,
As we forgive our debtors.

—MATTHEW 6:12 NKJV

*The longer I live, the more I realize how much
forgiveness I need from you, how much we all need.
My hidden sins of pride, envy, malice, hypocrisy, and
greed are no less spiritually deadly than promiscuity,
lying, adultery, and murder. There are no "safe" sins.
They may have different consequences, but they all
cost you the same painful price when you reached out
to offer forgiveness to all who would receive it. I have,
indeed, been forgiven much. May my love for you and
others reflect that I truly understand this.*

The humility that a forgiven person carries
is an approachable gentleness, a strength that
does not tolerate sentimental nonsense but loves
truthful tenderness. Facade cannot keep up
its pretenses in the presence of such humility,
but honest souls thrive in its presence. It is the
reflection of Christ's own truth and love.

Father, your Word says there is great rejoicing in heaven over one repentant sinner. I sometimes wonder what that tumult of celestial joy looks like. Was there one of those heavenly parties for me when I turned to you for forgiveness and a new start? That's something to think about (with a smile on my face). Now that I think about it, there must have been multiple parties for the times I've strayed and found myself needing to turn around. How consistent your grace has been, how continual your willingness to forgive! And not with a sigh of frustration either. You delight when I turn back to you, not because you are desperate for my love, but because you know how much I need yours.

Blessed is the one whose transgressions are forgiven . . . whose sin the Lord does not count against them and in whose spirit is no deceit.

—PSALM 32:1–2 NIV

*H*ow quiet my soul is after the storm of my fighting against what's right and true has ended and I've returned to you and received your forgiveness. The peace of restored fellowship with you is like nothing else. Why do I ever resist you? You never require me to stay, but I always want to come back. You truly are my shelter, my home, Lord. Thank you for forgiving me once again and for loving me still.

Father, you know that forgiveness does not come naturally to human hearts. We tend to maximize our grievances while minimizing our transgressions. That's why you call us over and over again to forgive— because we have been forgiven. It's only in being repeatedly reminded of my own need for forgiveness that I realize I must learn to forgive. So even though it is not my inclination to forgive, I want to develop a habit of sincerely forgiving others. Will you help me? Will you supply the strength of your love and the power of your Spirit to move me to forgive when I feel I cannot? Will you complete what is lacking in my heart so that I can forgive from the heart, as you tell me to do? I know I am praying within your will when I ask these things. So I'm confident and grateful for your answer.

The peace of a restored relationship
with God is never more than a repentant heart
and a sincere prayer away. We feel as though it
shouldn't be that simple, but it is.

It's not just the big things that others do that are hard to forgive, Lord. When it's someone I'm around daily, their irksome habits, which might actually be mere molehills, become towering peaks in my eyes. Especially thoughtless actions or omissions—things I've mentioned once or twice before and yet nothing changes—these things seem almost cruel to me at

times, and resentment sets in and begins to grow with
every "violation" of my expressed wishes. Lord, I need
to learn to let go of these small things, to look for
reasons and ways to love. Instead of focusing on what
people fail to do, help me recount their kindnesses and
the things they have done to be helpful and supportive.
Rather than being quick to accuse, lead me into a
heart that readily forgives.

Forgiveness is an act of the will, and the
will can function regardless of the
temperature of the heart.

—CORRIE TEN BOOM, *THE HIDING PLACE*

All the prophets testify about him that everyone
who believes in him receives forgiveness of sins
through his name.

—ACTS 10:43

If we can learn to readily forgive others
when they fail to meet our expectations,
forgiving ourselves when we miss
the mark becomes much easier.

*W*hen I wake up on the wrong side of the bed,
Lord, and launch into my day stomping around,
clouding up other people's sunny skies, help me not
resist your call (when I finally hear it) to stop, turn
around, ask forgiveness from you and the ones I've
trampled, and start over again. Please forgive my
pride when I've plugged my ears to your promptings
and refused to humble myself. I don't want to be
a person who is too arrogant to admit when I'm
off track. Help me be one who is quick to repent,
confess, and become grace-filled once again.

When pride wins the day, everyone loses.
But when humility prevails, among its rewards
are the love and respect we crave.

But I say to you that listen, Love your enemies, do good to those who hate you.

—Luke 6:27

Forgiveness is freedom, Lord, wonderful freedom! Will you help me take an inventory today to see if there is anyone I need to forgive? I don't want there to be any shadowy corners of unforgiveness anywhere in my heart. Open my eyes to grudges and grievances that I need to let go. If there is a conversation I need to have with someone to ask their forgiveness, help me see that, too. I want to live as freely as possible in the forgiveness you call me to walk in.

Forgiving a wrong is one of the "rightest" things we can do in this life.

And whenever you stand praying, if you have anything against anyone, forgive him, that your Father
in heaven may also forgive you your trespasses.

—MARK 11:25 NKJV

*T*he story in your Word, Lord, about the servant
who was forgiven a great debt by his master and yet
would not forgive his fellow servant a very small debt,
is a powerful reminder. It shows me plainly my need
to be forgiven as well as my obligation to forgive.
Help me never forget the magnitude of my debt you've
graciously wiped away so that I don't ever imagine that
I am above forgiving any wrong committed against
me. Today, help me truly rejoice in my salvation so
I'll be ready at a moment's notice to extend forgiveness
to another.

The key to forgiving others will always be
in realizing what we've already been forgiven.
When that happens, forgiveness becomes
primarily an act of gratitude to God.

Sometimes, Father, the shame and pain of past regrets can ambush my thoughts and emotions. When that happens, it doesn't take long for me to turn against myself with feelings of self-loathing and anger. The next step in my downward spiral is that I start lashing out at those around me—especially those closest to me. Oh, Father! How futile that sequence of turmoil is when you've fully forgiven me for my past transgressions! Please stop me when I begin to revisit what you have chosen to wash away. Help me look myself in the eye and say, "Your heavenly Father loves you and has forgiven you.  *You are forgiven. Now it's time to forgive yourself and live as one set free." Thank you for the freedom you hold out to me. Help me fully take hold of it.*

I think that if God forgives us we must forgive ourselves. Otherwise, it is almost like setting up ourselves as a higher tribunal than Him.

—C. S. LEWIS,
Letters of C. S. Lewis

Lord, your Word says that the same way we measure out grace and mercy to others is the way it will be measured back to us. So I ask myself today: Am I using the one-cup heaping full measure or am I reaching for the quarter teaspoon when I deal out forgiveness and mercy to the people around me? Oh, Lord! Help me be generous in love—generous to everyone at all times. For your glory . . . and for my own good.

[Jesus said,] "Do not judge, and you will not be judged. Do not condemn, and you will not be condemned. Forgive, and you will be forgiven."

—LUKE 6:37 NIV

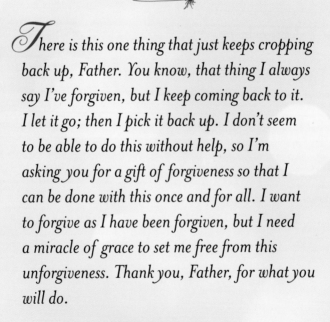

There is this one thing that just keeps cropping back up, Father. You know, that thing I always say I've forgiven, but I keep coming back to it. I let it go; then I pick it back up. I don't seem to be able to do this without help, so I'm asking you for a gift of forgiveness so that I can be done with this once and for all. I want to forgive as I have been forgiven, but I need a miracle of grace to set me free from this unforgiveness. Thank you, Father, for what you will do.

Sometimes the places we are stuck in spiritually
need miracles no less powerful or significant
than the ones by which the blind were cured,
the lepers were made whole, and the
dead were raised to life again.

The unpardonable sin requires a persistent, blatant rejection of God's truth, his call to repentance, and his offer of saving grace.

*L*ord, I know I have wondered about the "unpardonable sin" you mentioned—blaspheming the Holy Spirit. Thank you for helping me understand that to be guilty of that sin I'd have to be completely calloused to you, your Word, and your Spirit. Thank you for the sensitivity you've given my heart to the spiritual realities that are bound up in the truth of who you are. While I still stumble into sin on a daily basis, you've made me able to know the prompting of your Spirit, which guides me back to you. Because of that, I know the unpardonable sin isn't one I will stumble into. Thank you for assuring me again of your patience and love.

Some people have tried to tell me that there are many ways to find spiritual fulfillment. But I always feel my need to be forgiven and my sense that I can never do enough good things to erase my debt of sin. That's why I choose to call on you; you're the one who offers forgiveness, who pays my debt, who sets me free. I will praise you for that gift as long as I live. I am forgiven. I don't have to try to earn my way to you. You accept me, and you give me your Spirit to help me live well. I'm saved by your grace. Thank you!

Good works cannot save us, only God's mercy can do that. But once we have been forgiven, the desire to show gratitude for God's mercy comes out in good works.

Follow God's example, therefore, as dearly loved children and walk in the way of love, just as Christ loved us and gave himself up for us as a fragrant offering and sacrifice to God.

—Ephesians 5:1–2 NIV

My transgressions shout at me throughout the day, Lord. When I'm selfish, when I lose my temper, when I show a flash of arrogance . . . how it pains me! But when I cry out to you and ask you to forgive me and help me do better, the voice of conviction that has been correcting me quiets down and I hear your voice of welcome, forgiveness, and encouragement to try again. Thank you for both voices, but especially for that second one that grants me mercy and another chance.

The voice of sin is loud, but the
voice of forgiveness is louder.

—D. L. MOODY

CHAPTER 10

An Attitude
of Gratitude

And whatever you do, in word or
deed, do everything in the name
of the Lord Jesus, giving thanks to
God the Father through him.

—Colossians 3:17

God, I am thankful for everything that comes my way. I've lived long enough to learn that no matter what happens, good or bad, there is a blessing and a lesson to be learned, if I only take the time to look for them. I am grateful for the people, events, and experiences in my life that have made me who I am. I am also grateful, God, for all the amazing blessings yet to come.

Be filled with the Spirit, as you sing psalms and hymns and spiritual songs among yourselves, singing and making melody to the Lord in your hearts, giving thanks to God the Father at all times.

—Ephesians 5:18–20

It's easy to be grateful for the good things, but not so easy to thank God for the bad things. In happy times, we often forget to pray at all, thinking the good will last forever. Then the tide turns, and we are back asking God for help and comfort and never once thinking that perhaps we should be just as thankful for the experiences that are unfolding. We will never move outside of our comfort zone and learn the vital lessons of a life well lived if we don't accept the bumps in the road. Be thankful for all of it, because it all conspires to make us better, stronger, and wiser.

God never promises to remove us
from our struggles. He does promise,
however, to change the way we look at them.

—MAX LUCADO

How thankful I feel today, God, for the simple warmth of the sun on my skin and the sound of birds in the trees. How thankful I feel today for the smiles of people I meet along the way, for my car starting, and for my job that pays the bills. How thankful I feel today, dear God, for my friends and my family and for the people I work with. Sometimes my heart just wants to burst with blessings I've received and all the wonderful miracles that make ordinary life so extraordinary. How thankful I feel today, God, just to be alive! Amen.

If the only prayer you said was thank you,
that would be enough.

—MEISTER ECKHART

I can do all things through him who strengthens me.

—Philippians 4:13

When we change something as simple as our perception or attitude, our entire world is changed. Having an attitude of gratitude keeps our focus on the good in life and brings more good our way as a result.

$\mathscr{G}$ratitude is an attitude that anyone can adopt. You don't need to be tall or short, pretty or thin, athletic or spiritual. Anyone can have a grateful spirit and see the amazing and positive changes it brings. Being thankful for everything seems to open up the floodgates to even more things to be thankful for, and suddenly life feels like a joyful adventure and a blessed journey. Sure, we may be lacking for material things, but if we continue to look to the things we don't lack, our attitude will shift into a deeper state of grace. It doesn't take money or effort, just a little adjustment in how we look at what we are blessed with.

There are those days, Lord, when I can find little to be thankful for. Nothing goes as planned or is on time, and everyone gets under my skin and on my last nerve. These are the days I just want to crawl back into bed and hide. But then someone will smile at me, or act with kindness, or I'll see a beautiful garden on my way to work or the store . . . and it all comes back to me, Lord. All the reasons why this really is such a wonderful world full of things to thank you for. So thank you, Lord. Amen.

A grateful heart is one that finds the countless blessings of God in the seemingly mundane everyday life.

—ANONYMOUS

Oh, give thanks to the Lord, for He is good!
For His mercy endures forever.

—Psalm 136:1 NKJV

When I am feeling lost and alone and tired from the challenges of the day, I can always rely on a friend to lift my spirits, make me laugh, and help me forget my troubles, even if just for a short time. I think that is why God invented friendship—so that when we can't make it on our own, we have a group of people who can help ease our burdens and lighten our load. I am forever grateful for each of my friends, the old and the new, the ones who passed through for a while, and the ones who remain. Each of them has blessed me with their presence, and I'm grateful.

At times our own light goes out and is rekindled by a spark from another person. Each of us has cause to think with deep gratitude of those who have lighted the flame within us.

—ALBERT SCHWEITZER

I know it's a day like any other, God, but I am just glad to be alive. There were times in the past when I didn't even want to wake up and face the day, but now I realize how precious life is and how important each moment is. Thank you for instilling in me a wellspring of gratitude that I can dip into anytime I feel like life is drying up around me. I am blessed to be able to rise again in joy and good health and share it with those I love. I promise, God, to never take my life, or the precious moments that make up my days, for granted again!

It is only with gratitude that
life becomes rich.

—DIETRICH BONHOEFFER

**Therefore, since we are receiving a kingdom that
cannot be shaken, let us be thankful, and so
worship God acceptably with reverence and awe.**

—HEBREWS 12:28 NIV

*Whoever could imagine that being diagnosed with
cancer would be something to be grateful for? But it
happens to so many men and women who hear those
dreaded words from their doctor, thus beginning
a journey from fear and illness into resilience and
wholeness again. For some, the diagnosis may be
too late, but for those who are survivors, a common*

thread to their stories is the belief that what did not kill them made them stronger and helped rebuild their faith. To come out of the pit of darkness and be grateful for the experience is the gift of trials and setbacks. Life looks different to those who have been to hell and back. Life is precious and a gift to be ever thankful for.

In the midst of pain and suffering,
there appears on the surface to be nothing
worthy of our gratitude. But once we come back
into the light, we see how the experience
has changed us for the better.

Dear God, tonight as I turn to sleep, let me look back upon this day with a sense of completion and acceptance. What happened cannot "unhappen," and I am thankful for every moment just as it was. I know that when I was younger I longed to go back and change things that didn't turn out as I had planned or hoped. Now I am older and wiser, and I know that everything happens just as it should, just as you will it to. I may not always know the reason, but I know that it all happens for a reason. Help me accept it all, let it go, and look forward to a brand new day tomorrow. Amen.

**O give thanks to the Lord, for he is good;
for his steadfast love endures forever.**

—PSALM 107:1

I am human, hear me whine! Yes, it is so much easier to find things to complain about some days. But if I look a little deeper, I can find something to be happy about. It often starts with just saying a simple "thank you" to someone who helped me in some small way, and then maybe a smile followed, and a sense of feeling good about people, and before I know it, I am a little lighter on my feet. In the midst of my moaning and groaning about life, if I stop, just STOP, and thank God for the first thing I see, that leads to being thankful for other things, and soon the list snowballs and I am grateful for everything. It all begins with two words—"thank you"—to turn my whine into feeling fine.

The simple act of saying "thank you"
to one thing opens the heart to so many
other things to be grateful for.
Gratitude multiplies our blessings!

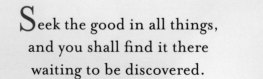

Seek the good in all things,
and you shall find it there
waiting to be discovered.
A grateful heart finds treasure in everything.

Imagine what your life would be like if you started each day asking, "What can I be grateful for today?" With open eyes and an open heart, you would approach each event, circumstance, and person with an attitude of finding the best in them, instead of automatically assuming the worst. Everything that happens would be a new opportunity to find the gift or the lesson, and no cloud would escape the search for a silver lining. Imagine what your life would be like if you ended each day with a prayer of thanks to God, telling him all that you found to be grateful for!

Let the word of Christ dwell in you richly; teach and admonish one another in all wisdom; and with gratitude in your hearts sing psalms, hymns, and spiritual songs to God.

—COLOSSIANS 3:16

Lord, I ask to be forgiven for all the times I took the amazing blessings in my life for granted. So often I just accept that I can have this or that, and I forget that there are so many others less fortunate out there, living on so much less. I don't ever want to take one thing for granted, even those things that bring me sadness and despair, because it all adds up to a life deeply lived. Please forgive me when I act spoiled or entitled, and remind me to walk with grace and humility. I know that all I have can be taken away, and I don't want to become dependent on the material things. I only want to depend on you, Lord, and on the things money can't buy. Thank you, Lord.

Never take a moment for granted,
or a person or thing or event. Everything we are
blessed with is something to be celebrated
and grateful for. Everything.

What is it about birdsong that makes me feel so happy? What is it about the warm sun and the swaying trees that open my heart to the wonders of this world? How can I look around at nature and not realize how blessed I am to be alive? Gratitude isn't *always about being thankful for the things I have and the people I love, but about the world around me, with all its minor and major miracles. Can you gaze at a starry night sky and not feel the grandeur? Can you stand before the mighty ocean and not feel pure awe? I certainly can't. Thank you, God, for your creation.*

Shout for joy to the Lord, all the earth.
Worship the Lord with gladness;
come before him with joyful songs.
Know that the Lord is God.
It is he who made us, and we are his;
we are his people, the sheep of his pasture.
Enter his gates with thanksgiving
and his courts with praise;
give thanks to him and praise his name.

—PSALM 100:1–4

*W*isdom and experience teach us to look for the good in the bad. Being thankful for even the most difficult of trials or the biggest of obstacles can be an act of revelation, in which we discover a gem of a lesson hidden in the midst of chaos. The older we get, the easier it is to see the gem and embrace it, and come to a place of acceptance. It will get better. This too shall pass. Today is always followed by tomorrow. Even if that is the only lesson we glean from our suffering, it is enough.

Time teaches us to accept everything that happens to us as an opportunity for our own personal growth and understanding. There is always something new to learn.

Father above, I am at a point in my life where everything is OK. Not perfect but good enough, and for that I am grateful. It's not so much what I have, God, as finding a way to be happy with it. I know I could be more and do more and have more, but this is where I want to be, right now, and it feels great to just accept that. Life doesn't have to be all about striving. It can be about arriving, right where you stand today. Thank you, Father God, for helping me see that I don't need anything to be different now that I see it all differently.

If we always want more than what we have,
we can rest assured we will never be happy.
If we can find a way to want what we have
already been given, happiness comes easily.

You are my God, and I will praise You;
You are my God, I will exalt You.
Oh, give thanks to the Lord, for He is
good! For His mercy endures forever.

—Psalm 118:28–29 NKJV

Lord, I've prayed for healing and hope,
comfort and love, faith and strength. But
rarely have I stopped long enough in my
asking to say thanks for my receiving. I've
asked for more money, less pain, more
peace, less stress, but how often have I just
prayed to give praise and thanks for all you have done
for me? Today I pray only to say that I am grateful
beyond words for the prayers you've answered, and
even the ones you haven't, because I know that your
will has always been what is best for me. Thank you,
Lord. Thank you.

———— ✳ ————

Life itself is the greatest gift of all, yet too often we walk through our days in a fog, not aware or awake to the miracles that surround us . . . until it is too late. Don't let it be too late. Give thanks to God for this day, now!

———— ✳ ————

Just the fact that you are still breathing is something to be grateful for. Just being given the gift of another day is precious, because there are those who will be called home to God today. We take a lot of things for granted, but most of all we take life for granted. Each breath should be treated like gold, and each morning we rise should be recognized as a whole new opportunity to do things differently, live more presently, and spend our time more wisely.

G̲od gave you a gift of
86,400 seconds today. Have you used
one to say, "Thank you"?

—WILLIAM WARD

So then, just as you received Christ Jesus as Lord, continue to live your lives in him, rooted and built up in him, strengthened in the faith as you were taught, and overflowing with thankfulness.

—Colossians 2:6–7 NIV

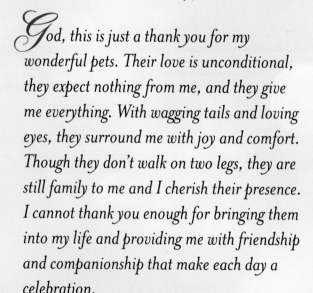

God, this is just a thank you for my wonderful pets. Their love is unconditional, they expect nothing from me, and they give me everything. With wagging tails and loving eyes, they surround me with joy and comfort. Though they don't walk on two legs, they are still family to me and I cherish their presence. I cannot thank you enough for bringing them into my life and providing me with friendship and companionship that make each day a celebration.

Pets are like family, without the drama and bickering! Pets are best friends and confidantes, companions and dream partners. Pets are pieces of God with love in their eyes. Hug your pet today!

Dear Lord, today I praise you for just being in my life. No matter what is happening, your presence is here, standing beside me, helping me make the best choices and do the right thing in any situation. I feel your constant comfort, your guiding wisdom, and your merciful love each and every moment of the day, giving me the courage to move forward in life even when met with obstacles along my path. I pray today only to thank you, Lord, with every fiber of my being, for being there for me. Amen.

Just knowing that we are never alone as we go through life is reason enough for celebration and thanksgiving.

Make a joyful noise to God, all the earth; sing the
glory of his name; give to him glorious praise. Say
to God, "How awesome are your deeds!"

—PSALM 66:1–3